CAMBRIDGE SCHOOL

Shakespeare

The Merchant of Venice

Edited by Jonathan Morris and Robert Smith

Series Editor: Rex Gibson
Director, Shakespeare and Schools Project

CAMBRIDGE
UNIVERSITY PRESS

PUBLISHED BY THE PRESS SYNDICATE OF THE UNIVERSITY OF CAMBRIDGE
The Pitt Building, Trumpington Street, Cambridge, United Kingdom

CAMBRIDGE UNIVERSITY PRESS
The Edinburgh Building, Cambridge CB2 2RU, UK   http://www.cup.cam.ac.uk
40 West 20th Street, New York, NY 10011–4211, USA   http://www.cup.org
10 Stamford Road, Oakleigh, Melbourne 3166, Australia
Ruiz de Alarcón 13, 28014 Madrid, Spain

First published 1992
Eighth printing 1999

Printed in the United Kingdom at the University Press, Cambridge

Typeface   M Ehrhardt

A catalogue record for this book is available from the British Library

Library of Congress Cataloguing in Publication data applied for

ISBN 0 521 42504 2 paperback

Prepared for publication by Stenton Associates
Designed by Richard Morris, Stonedfield Design
Picture research by Callie Kendall

Contents

Cambridge School Shakespeare

This edition of *The Merchant of Venice* is part of the *Cambridge School Shakespeare* series. Like every other play in the series, it has been specially prepared to help all students in schools and colleges.

This *The Merchant of Venice* aims to be different from other editions of the play. It invites you to bring the play to life in your classroom, hall or drama studio through enjoyable activities that will increase your understanding. Actors have created their different interpretations of the play over the centuries. Similarly, you are encouraged to make up your own mind about *The Merchant of Venice*, rather than having someone else's interpretation handed down to you.

Cambridge School Shakespeare does not offer you a cut-down or simplified version of the play. This is Shakespeare's language, filled with imaginative possibilities. You will find on every left-hand page: a summary of the action, an explanation of unfamiliar words, a choice of activities on Shakespeare's language, characters and stories.

Between each act and in the pages at the end of the play, you will find notes, illustrations and activities. These will help to increase your understanding of the whole play.

There are a large number of activities to give you the widest choice to suit your own particular needs. Please don't think you have to do every one. Choose the activities that will help you most.

This edition will be of value to you whether you are studying for an examination, reading for pleasure, or thinking of putting on the play to entertain others. You can work on the activities on your own or in groups. Many of the activities suggest a particular group size, but don't be afraid to make up larger or smaller groups to suit your own purposes.

Although you are invited to treat *The Merchant of Venice* as a play, you don't need special dramatic or theatrical skills to do the activities. By choosing your activities, and by exploring and experimenting, you can make your own interpretations of Shakespeare's language, characters and stories. Whatever you do, remember that Shakespeare wrote his plays to be acted, watched and enjoyed.

Rex Gibson

This edition of *The Merchant of Venice* uses the text of the play established by M. M. Mahood in *The New Cambridge Shakespeare.*

List of characters

Venice

Christians

THE DUKE OF VENICE

BASSANIO, a lord
ANTONIO, a merchant
SOLANIO
SALARINO
GRATIANO } Friends of Antonio and Bassanio
SALERIO
LORENZO

LANCELOT GOBBO, servant first
   to Shylock, then to Bassanio
GOBBO, his father
STEPHANO, a messenger
JAILER
LEONARDO, servant of Bassanio
SERVINGMAN, employed by
   Antonio
MAGNIFICOES OF VENICE
COURT OFFICIALS

Jews

SHYLOCK, a rich money-lender
JESSICA, his daughter
TUBAL, his friend

Belmont

Portia's household

PORTIA, a rich heiress
NERISSA, her lady-in-waiting
BALTHAZAR, her servant
SERVINGMAN
MESSENGER

Portia's suitors

THE PRINCE OF MOROCCO
THE PRINCE OF ARRAGON

The action of the play takes place in Venice and Belmont.

The Merchant of Venice

Antonio says he does not know what causes his sadness. Salarino and Solanio suggest that he is worried about the safety of his ships, in which he has invested so much money.

1 Where are they? (in pairs)

Shakespeare left no stage directions to show the exact location of each scene. On the Elizabethan stage the action flowed swiftly from scene to scene without the aid of an elaborate set. Since Shakespeare's day, each editor of the play, and each director of a stage production, takes decisions about whether they will indicate precise locations. So try your hand at scene-setting. Decide on a suitable place in Venice for the three friends' meeting. Perhaps they meet in a house or an office, or in a public place such as a bar, a café or the Stock Exchange. Give reasons for your choice.

2 Before the play begins (in groups of three)

The play begins in the middle of a conversation. Improvise how you think the talking would have begun.

3 Waiting for the ships

In lines 15–22 Solanio describes nervously waiting for the safe outcome of a trade deal involving transport by sea. What gestures or actions would you suggest to an actor to accompany his speech? Show your ideas to the rest of the class. The following explanations will help you:

'Plucking . . . wind' throwing grass in the air to find the direction of the wind
'piring' looking closely at
'roads' anchorages

---

sooth truth
to . . . learn ignorant
And . . . myself sadness has made me so absent-minded that I hardly know who I am
argosies merchant ships
portly stately

signors gentlemen
burghers important citizens
pageants processions
Do . . . traffickers look down on small boats
do them . . . reverence show them respect

2

The Merchant of Venice

ACT I   SCENE I
Venice

Enter ANTONIO, SALARINO, and SOLANIO

ANTONIO In sooth I know not why I am so sad.
　　　　It wearies me, you say it wearies you;
　　　　But how I caught it, found it, or came by it,
　　　　What stuff 'tis made of, whereof it is born,
　　　　I am to learn.   5
　　　　And such a want-wit sadness makes of me,
　　　　That I have much ado to know myself.
SALARINO Your mind is tossing on the ocean,
　　　　There where your argosies with portly sail
　　　　Like signors and rich burghers on the flood,   10
　　　　Or as it were the pageants of the sea,
　　　　Do overpeer the petty traffickers
　　　　That curtsey to them, do them reverence,
　　　　As they fly by them with their woven wings.
SOLANIO Believe me, sir, had I such venture forth,   15
　　　　The better part of my affections would
　　　　Be with my hopes abroad. I should be still
　　　　Plucking the grass to know where sits the wind,
　　　　Piring in maps for ports, and piers, and roads;
　　　　And every object that might make me fear   20
　　　　Misfortune to my ventures, out of doubt
　　　　Would make me sad.

Antonio says he is not worried about business matters. He has invested his money in several ships. That is much safer than relying on only one. He's not in love either!

1 The dangers of the sea

Salarino says that if he were in Antonio's situation, everything he did or saw would constantly remind him of what disasters might happen to his ships. Even blowing his soup to cool it would make him think of tempests. Lines 22–36 are full of images of calamity at sea.

Either Choose your favourite image from Salarino's lines. Design a picture to show it.

Or (in groups of four) Make up a short play. A business person is worried about the safe arrival of some valuable goods. The problem is that everything she sees or does reminds her of possible disaster to her cargo.

Antonio's argosy? A galleon similar to the trading ships of Venice. Why were such vessels so vulnerable to accidents at sea?

2 I'm not love-sick!

Antonio reacts unfavourably to the suggestion that he might be in love ('Fie, fie!'). What does this suggest to you about him and his attitude to women?

---

wealthy Andrew the *San Andres* (St Andrew), a valuable Spanish ship captured by the English in 1596
vailing ... top bowing down her mainmast

holy ... stone the font
Janus a Roman god who faced in two opposite directions
Nestor a Greek king, famed for his seriousness

SALARINO   My wind cooling my broth
    Would blow me to an ague when I thought
    What harm a wind too great might do at sea.
    I should not see the sandy hourglass run   25
    But I should think of shallows and of flats,
    And see my wealthy Andrew docked in sand,
    Vailing her high top lower than her ribs
    To kiss her burial. Should I go to church
    And see the holy edifice of stone   30
    And not bethink me straight of dangerous rocks,
    Which touching but my gentle vessel's side
    Would scatter all her spices on the stream,
    Enrobe the roaring waters with my silks,
    And (in a word) but even now worth this,   35
    And now worth nothing? Shall I have the thought
    To think on this, and shall I lack the thought
    That such a thing bechanced would make me sad?
    But tell not me: I know Antonio
    Is sad to think upon his merchandise.   40
ANTONIO Believe me, no. I thank my fortune for it,
    My ventures are not in one bottom trusted,
    Nor to one place; nor is my whole estate
    Upon the fortune of this present year:
    Therefore my merchandise makes me not sad.   45
SOLANIO Why then, you are in love.
ANTONIO   Fie, fie!
SOLANIO Not in love neither? Then let us say you are sad
    Because you are not merry; and 'twere as easy
    For you to laugh and leap, and say you are merry
    Because you not sad. Now by two-headed Janus,   50
    Nature hath framed strange fellows in her time:
    Some that will evermore peep through their eyes,
    And laugh like parrots at a bagpiper;
    And other of such vinegar aspèct,
    That they'll not show their teeth in way of smile   55
    Though Nestor swear the jest be laughable.

*More friends arrive. One of them, Gratiano, comments on how careworn
Antonio has become. He recommends laughter over misery and
warns against false seriousness.*

1 Real friends? (in pairs)

Solanio and Salarino decide to leave when the other friends of
Antonio arrive. But why?

Read their lines 57–68 to see if there are any clues to their sudden
exit. Try reading the lines aloud in different tones of voice. Are these
words as friendly and polite as they appear?

Work on what the two men say about their talk with Antonio.
Improvise their conversation after they leave him.

2 All the world's a stage (in pairs)

Antonio's lines 77–9 echo well-known words from Shakespeare's *As
You Like It*:

All the world's a stage,
And all the men and women merely players:
They have their exits and their entrances;
And one man in his time plays many parts.

Talk together about the differences between these four lines and
what Antonio says. What does it tell you about him and his view of
life?

3 Sir Oracle

In lines 88–94, Gratiano makes fun of those who take themselves too
seriously and pretend they are very wise. He even invents Sir Oracle,
a caricature of such a person. Draw your version of Gratiano's
creation.

Your ... regard you're a good
  friend
We'll ... yours our time is yours
strange unfriendly
You ... world you care too much
  about what people think
And ... groans I'd rather cheer
  myself up with drink than weaken
  my heart with sighs and being
  miserable

Sit ... alabaster be like his
  grandfather's statue in the
  cemetery
visages faces
Do cream ... and mantle become
  still and covered over
oracle someone of infinite wisdom

Enter BASSANIO, LORENZO, *and* GRATIANO

Here comes Bassanio, your most noble kinsman,
Gratiano, and Lorenzo. Fare ye well;
We leave you now with better company.

SALARINO I would have stayed till I had made you merry,   60
If worthier friends had not prevented me.

ANTONIO Your worth is very dear in my regard.
I take it your own business calls on you,
And you embrace th'occasion to depart.

SALARINO Good morrow, my good lords.   65

BASSANIO Good signors both, when shall we laugh? Say, when?
You grow exceeding strange; must it be so?

SALARINO We'll make our leisures to attend on yours.
           Exeunt Salarino and Solanio

LORENZO My Lord Bassanio, since you have found Antonio
We two will leave you, but at dinner time   70
I pray you have in mind where we must meet.

BASSANIO I will not fail you.

GRATIANO You look not well, Signor Antonio.
You have too much respect upon the world:
They lose it that do buy it with much care.   75
Believe me, you are marvellously changed.

ANTONIO I hold the world but as the world, Gratiano:
A stage where every man must play a part,
And mine a sad one.

GRATIANO   Let me play the Fool.
With mirth and laughter let old wrinkles come,   80
And let my liver rather heat with wine
Than my heart cool with mortifying groans.
Why should a man whose blood is warm within
Sit like his grandsire cut in alabaster?
Sleep when he wakes? And creep into the jaundice   85
By being peevish? I tell thee what, Antonio –
I love thee, and it is my love that speaks –
There are a sort of men whose visages
Do cream and mantle like a standing pond,
And do a wilful stillness entertain,   90
With purpose to be dressed in an opinion
Of wisdom, gravity, profound conceit,
As who should say, 'I am Sir Oracle,
And when I ope my lips, let no dog bark!'

Gratiano advises Antonio against using sadness to gain a reputation for wisdom. Antonio asks Bassanio whom he loves. Bassanio begins by explaining his plans to pay off his debts.

1 Bassanio the back-stabber? (in pairs)

After Gratiano leaves, Bassanio comments on his character (lines 114–17). Are his words friendly or harsh? Read the lines to each other in different ways: jokingly, as a friend; and bitterly, as a harsh critic.

Then talk about what you think is Bassanio's true attitude to Gratiano.

2 Money, money, money (in groups of four to six)

Bassanio has been asked about love, but he begins his answer by talking about his debts. He has spent all his money and owes a great deal.

One person reads aloud lines 121–33. The others echo every word to do with money.

In a series of no more than five still images (tableaux) show how you think Bassanio might have got himself into so much financial trouble. Invent captions for each tableau to display or announce to your audience.

Talk together about what the lines tell you about Bassanio's personality.

That therefore . . . nothing whose silence gains them a reputation for wisdom
this . . . opinion this stupid fish called reputation
exhortation strongly offered advice
gear advice (or business)
neat's tongue ox tongue
vendible desirable
secret pilgrimage journey of love

By something . . . grant continuance by enjoying a standard of living I could not afford
Nor . . . rate I don't complain about having to economise
prodigal wasteful
gaged owing
And . . . purposes because of our friendship I owe you an explanation

O my Antonio, I do know of these   95
That therefore only are reputed wise
For saying nothing; when I am very sure
If they should speak, would almost damn those ears
Which, hearing them, would call their brothers fools.
I'll tell thee more of this another time.   100
But fish not with this melancholy bait
For this fool gudgeon, this opinion.
Come, good Lorenzo. Fare ye well awhile;
I'll end my exhortation after dinner.
LORENZO Well, we will leave you then till dinner time.   105
I must be one of these same dumb wise men,
For Gratiano never lets me speak.
GRATIANO Well, keep me company but two years moe,
Thou shalt not know the sound of thine own tongue.
ANTONIO Farewell; I'll grow a talker for this gear.   110
GRATIANO Thanks, i'faith, for silence is only commendable
In a neat's tongue dried, and a maid not vendible.
                         Exeunt [Gratiano and Lorenzo]
ANTONIO It is that anything now.
BASSANIO Gratiano speaks an infinite deal of nothing, more than any
man in all Venice. His reasons are as two grains of wheat hid in two   115
bushels of chaff: you shall seek all day ere you find them, and when
you have them they are not worth the search.
ANTONIO Well, tell me now what lady is the same
To whom you swore a secret pilgrimage
That you today promised to tell me of.   120
BASSANIO 'Tis not unknown to you, Antonio,
How much I have disabled mine estate
By something showing a more swelling port
Than my faint means would grant continuance.
Nor do I now make moan to be abridged   125
From such a noble rate, but my chief care
Is to come fairly off from the great debts
Wherein my time, something too prodigal,
Hath left me gaged. To you, Antonio,
I owe the most in money and in love,   130
And from your love I have a warranty
To unburden all my plots and purposes
How to get clear of all the debts I owe.

*Antonio is ready to help Bassanio, whatever the circumstances. Bassanio
explains that he wishes to marry Portia, a wealthy heiress. Rich and famous
men from all over the world come to woo her.*

1 Good money after bad? (in pairs)

Bassanio argues in lines 139–51 that if Antonio lends him more
money, he is more likely to be re-paid his earlier loan. Bassanio uses
the image of a lost arrow ('shaft') which might be found by shooting
another one in the same direction. Antonio is happy to accept this
argument, but would it convince you? Improvise a scene in which one
person tries to persuade the other to lend more money to help pay
back a previous debt between them.

2 First impressions of Portia (in small groups)

In lines 160–71 we first hear of Portia. Bassanio uses stories of
Ancient Greece and Rome to praise her. He compares her to 'Cato's
daughter, Brutus' Portia'. She was the daughter of Cato, a famous
Roman politician, and wife of Brutus, the 'honourable man' who was
one of Julius Caesar's assassins. Bassanio also sees her as a rich prize,
like the Golden Fleece the Greek hero Jason sought in Colchis.
These references would have been understood by educated members
of Shakespeare's audience. They also indicate Bassanio's own social
class.

Read aloud lines 160–71. Each person reads up to a punctuation
mark, then hands on. Emphasise all the words Bassanio uses to praise
Portia.

Write or draw your own impressions of Portia from Bassanio's
description.

Talk together about the effect Bassanio's classical references have
on his description of Portia.

And if ... honour and if it's
honourable, as you are
My purse ... occasions everything
I have is at your disposal
a wilful ... lost like a stupid boy,
I've lost every penny I've borrowed
from you

To wind ... circumstance to
make use of my love for you in a
roundabout way
prest unto forced into
a lady richly left a rich heiress

ANTONIO I pray you, good Bassanio, let me know it,
        And if it stand as you yourself still do   135
        Within the eye of honour, be assured
        My purse, my person, my extremest means
        Lie all unlocked to your occasions.
BASSANIO In my schooldays, when I had lost one shaft,
        I shot his fellow of the selfsame flight   140
        The selfsame way, with more advisèd watch
        To find the other forth; and by adventuring both
        I oft found both. I urge this childhood proof
        Because what follows is pure innocence.
        I owe you much, and like a wilful youth   145
        That which I owe is lost; but if you please
        To shoot another arrow that self way
        Which you did shoot the first, I do not doubt,
        As I will watch the aim, or to find both
        Or bring your latter hazard back again   150
        And thankfully rest debtor for the first.
ANTONIO You know me well, and herein spend but time
        To wind about my love with circumstance;
        And out of doubt you do me now more wrong
        In making question of my uttermost   155
        Than if you had made waste of all I have.
        Then do but say to me what I should do
        That in your knowledge may by me be done,
        And I am prest unto it: therefore speak.
BASSANIO In Belmont is a lady richly left,   160
        And she is fair, and – fairer than that word –
        Of wondrous virtues. Sometimes from her eyes
        I did receive fair speechless messages.
        Her name is Portia, nothing undervalued
        To Cato's daughter, Brutus' Portia.   165
        Nor is the wide world ignorant of her worth;
        For the four winds blow in from every coast
        Renownèd suitors, and her sunny locks
        Hang on her temples like a golden fleece,
        Which makes her seat of Belmont Colchos' strand,   170
        And many Jasons come in quest of her.

Antonio's cash is tied up in his ships, but he allows Bassanio to borrow money on his behalf. In Belmont, Portia complains that her dead father's will prevents her from choosing her own husband.

1 Bassanio's small ad

Bassanio places an advertisement in the *Venice Times*, asking to borrow money. He commissions you to write the advert. You have to persuade readers that the money will be wisely invested. He gives you permission to mention his social background, the involvement of Antonio, and how the money will be used.

2 Nerissa's wisdom: sixty-second theatre
(in groups of four or five)

Nerissa tells Portia that riches don't bring happiness:

> '. . . they are as sick that surfeit with too much as they that starve with nothing.'

Talk together about whether you think this might be Shakespeare's comment on the characters appearing in Scene 1. Then use Nerissa's words as the title for your own sixty-second theatre. Your play should be no longer than a minute, and must show Nerissa's words in action.

3 Giving advice . . . or following it?

It's easier to hand out good advice than to follow it, says Portia in lines 11–18. Identify the four or five ways in which she makes this point, then write advice for the actor playing Portia on how to make each illustration clear to the audience.

I . . . thrift I feel I'm going to make a huge profit
at sea invested in my ships
racked . . . to the uttermost stretched to the limit
presently immediately
To have . . . sake on my credit or for the sake of friendship
surfeit overfeed
seated in the mean of average wealth

superfluity . . . longer too much good living ages us; having just enough makes us live longer
divine priest
The brain . . . decree the head is overruled by the heart
meshes nets
But . . . husband all this talking won't help me find a man

O my Antonio, had I but the means
To hold a rival place with one of them,
I have a mind presages me such thrift
That I should questionless be fortunate.   175
ANTONIO Thou know'st that all my fortunes are at sea;
Neither have I money nor commodity
To raise a present sum; therefore go forth,
Try what my credit can in Venice do,
That shall be racked even to the uttermost   180
To furnish thee to Belmont to fair Portia.
Go presently enquire, and so will I,
Where money is, and I no question make
To have it of my trust or for my sake.   *Exeunt*

ACT 1   SCENE 2
Belmont   The garden of Portia's house

Enter PORTIA and NERISSA

PORTIA By my troth, Nerissa, my little body is aweary of this great
world.

NERISSA You would be, sweet madam, if your miseries were in the
same abundance as your good fortunes are; and yet for aught I see,
they are as sick that surfeit with too much as they that starve with   5
nothing. It is no mean happiness, therefore, to be seated in the
mean – superfluity comes sooner by white hairs, but competency
lives longer.

PORTIA Good sentences, and well pronounced.

NERISSA They would be better if well followed.   10

PORTIA If to do were as easy as to know what were good to do, chapels
had been churches, and poor men's cottages princes' palaces. It is
a good divine that follows his own instructions; I can easier teach
twenty what were good to be done, than be one of the twenty to
follow mine own teaching. The brain may devise laws for the   15
blood, but a hot temper leaps o'er a cold decree – such a hare is
madness the youth, to skip o'er the meshes of good counsel the
cripple. But this reasoning is not in the fashion to choose me a
husband. O me, the word 'choose'! I may neither choose who I
would, nor refuse who I dislike, so is the will of a living daughter   20
curbed by the will of a dead father. Is it not hard, Nerissa, that I
cannot choose one, nor refuse none?

*Nerissa recaps the will: potential husbands (suitors) must choose
between three caskets of gold, silver and lead. Whoever chooses correctly wins
Portia! Nerissa begins describing Portia's suitors.*

1 Portia's father

We are not told much about the former master of Belmont. What can
you deduce about him from lines 19–29?

Write a pen portrait of Portia's father. Compare your impressions
with those of other students.

2 The will

Portia's father has left a will, setting out the conditions for her
marriage. Make up a copy of the will, including the terms described in
lines 23–9. Try to use the language of a legal document.

3 Arranged marriages (in groups of four or five)

Marriages in which partners are chosen by the parents are a feature of
some modern societies. Make lists of the advantages and disadvantages of arranged marriages. Remember that many people feel that
arranged marriages are more stable and lasting than those in which
the partners choose each other.

4 Six suitors: a mini-pageant (in six groups)

Lines 30–81 describe Portia's six suitors. Each group takes a different
suitor:

- Devise a suitable coat of arms and motto for your choice.
- Experiment with ways of portraying your suitor, played by one of
  the group, according to Portia's description.
- Present your work to the rest of the class in mini-pageant form: the
  grand entry of your suitor and his followers to Belmont.

---

his meaning the one he intended
over-name list
level at guess
colt rough young man
and he makes it . . . himself he is
  proud of being able to shoe his own
  horse
played false had sex
he is . . . man he copies everyone,
  but has no personality of his own
throstle thrush
he falls . . . capering starts
  dancing about
requite him love him in return

NERISSA Your father was ever virtuous; and holy men at their death
have good inspirations. Therefore the lottery that he hath devised
in these three chests of gold, silver, and lead, whereof who chooses   25
his meaning chooses you, will no doubt never be chosen by any
rightly but one who you shall rightly love. But what warmth is
there in your affection towards any of these princely suitors that are
already come?

PORTIA I pray thee over-name them, and as thou namest them I will   30
describe them – and according to my description, level at my affection.

NERISSA First, there is the Neapolitan prince.

PORTIA Ay, that's a colt indeed, for he doth nothing but talk of his
horse; and he makes it a great appropriation to his own good parts   35
that he can shoe him himself. I am much afeared my lady his
mother played false with a smith.

NERISSA Then is there the County Palatine.

PORTIA He doth nothing but frown, as who should say, 'And you will
not have me, choose.' He hears merry tales and smiles not; I fear   40
he will prove the weeping philosopher when he grows old, being so
full of unmannerly sadness in his youth. I had rather be married to
a death's head with a bone in his mouth than to either of these. God
defend me from these two!

NERISSA How say you by the French lord, Monsieur Le Bon?   45

PORTIA God made him, and therefore let him pass for a man. In truth
I know it is a sin to be a mocker, but he! – why, he hath a horse
better than the Neapolitan's, a better bad habit of frowning than the
Count Palatine: he is every man in no man. If a throstle sing, he
falls straight a-capering; he will fence with his own shadow. If I   50
should marry him, I should marry twenty husbands. If he would
despise me, I would forgive him; for if he love me to madness, I
shall never requite him.

NERISSA What say you then to Falconbridge, the young baron of
England?   55

The two women end their mocking of Portia's suitors. Nerissa reports the men's intention to return home immediately. She reminds Portia of her past meeting with Bassanio.

Another suitor? King Philip of Spain visited London in 1564 to marry Queen Mary. Why did world leaders at that time prefer to have arranged marriages?

1 National stereotypes (in pairs)

In Shakespeare's time the suitors would have been recognised as national stereotypes: Italians were thought to be good with horses and Germans to be drunkards. Stereotyping is unfair and inaccurate, but it still goes on. Talk together about modern examples of national stereotyping in films or television programmes.

dumbshow a mimed play
borrowed . . . ear was punched on
  the ear
become his surety . . . another
  was also struck by the Englishman
  and swore to pay him back

determinations plans
Sibylla Roman prophetess (she
  could live as many years as she
  could hold grains of sand)
Diana goddess of chastity (virginity)
  and the Moon

PORTIA You know I say nothing to him, for he understands not me,
nor I him: he hath neither Latin, French, nor Italian, and you will
come into the court and swear that I have a poor penny-worth in
the English. He is a proper man's picture, but alas who can converse
with a dumbshow? How oddly he is suited! I think he bought his   60
doublet in Italy, his round hose in France, his bonnet in Germany,
and his behaviour everywhere.

NERISSA What think you of the Scottish lord his neighbour?

PORTIA That he hath a neighbourly charity in him, for he borrowed a
box of the ear of the Englishman and swore he would pay him again   65
when he was able. I think the Frenchman became his surety and
sealed under for another.

NERISSA How like you the young German, the Duke of Saxony's
nephew?

PORTIA Very vilely in the morning when he is sober, and most vilely   70
in the afternoon when he is drunk. When he is best he is a little
worse than a man, and when he is worst he is little better than a
beast. And the worst fall that ever fell, I hope I shall make shift to
go without him.

NERISSA If he should offer to choose, and choose the right casket, you 75
should refuse to perform your father's will if you should refuse to
accept him.

PORTIA Therefore, for fear of the worst, I pray thee set a deep glass of
Rhenish wine on the contrary casket, for if the devil be within, and
that temptation without, I know he will choose it. I will do any-   80
thing, Nerissa, ere I will be married to a sponge.

NERISSA You need not fear, lady, the having any of these lords. They
have acquainted me with their determinations, which is indeed to
return to their home, and to trouble you with no more suit unless
you may be won by some other sort than your father's imposition,   85
depending on the caskets.

PORTIA If I live to be as old as Sibylla, I will die as chaste as Diana
unless I be obtained by the manner of my father's will. I am glad
this parcel of wooers are so reasonable, for there is not one among
them but I dote on his very absence; and I pray God grant them   90
a fair departure.

NERISSA Do you not remember, lady, in your father's time, a Venetian,
a scholar and a soldier, that came hither in company of the Marquis
of Montferrat?

*...servant announces that the suitors are about to leave, and that another,
the Prince of Morocco, will soon arrive. In Venice, Bassanio tries to
borrow money from Shylock.*

1 Spot the mistake!

The servingman gets something wrong. What is it?

2 End of the scene (in pairs)

The servant enters at the moment when Portia seems to be about to
say more about Bassanio.

Read lines 95–9 to each other in different ways to see if you can
guess Portia's feelings for Bassanio.

Why has Shakespeare chosen not to allow Portia to tell of her
feelings about Bassanio, but introduced the Prince of Morocco
instead?

3 Choose a location (in groups of four or five)

Talk together about a suitable place in Venice for this business
meeting between Bassanio and Shylock. Share your ideas with the
rest of the class. What reasons do you have for your choice ?

4 Enter Bassanio with Shylock (in pairs)

Once again we meet characters in the middle of a conversation. Read
lines 1–11 to catch the gist of what they are discussing, then
improvise their meeting before line 1.

---

forerunner a messenger
condition character
complexion . . . devil Elizabethans
  believed that devils were black
I had . . . wive me I would rather
  he be my priest than my husband

sirrah my man
ducats gold coins, coins of the
  duke
shall be bound will have to repay
Have . . . contrary? Have you
  heard differently?

PORTIA Yes, yes, it was Bassanio! – as I think so was he called. 95

NERISSA True, madam; he of all the men that ever my foolish eyes looked upon was the best deserving a fair lady.

PORTIA I remember him well, and I remember him worthy of thy praise.

Enter a SERVINGMAN

How now, what news? 100

SERVINGMAN The four strangers seek for you, madam, to take their leave; and there is a forerunner come from a fifth, the Prince of Morocco, who brings word the prince his master will be here tonight.

PORTIA If I could bid the fifth welcome with so good heart as I can bid 105 the other four farewell, I should be glad of his approach. If he have the condition of a saint, and the complexion of a devil, I had rather he should shrive me than wive me.
Come, Nerissa; sirrah, go before:
Whiles we shut the gate upon one wooer, another knocks at 110 the door

Exeunt

ACT 1   SCENE 3
Venice

Enter BASSANIO with SHYLOCK the Jew

SHYLOCK Three thousand ducats, well.

BASSANIO Ay, sir, for three months.

SHYLOCK For three months, well.

BASSANIO For the which, as I told you, Antonio shall be bound.

SHYLOCK Antonio shall become bound, well. 5

BASSANIO May you stead me? Will you pleasure me? Shall I know your answer?

SHYLOCK Three thousand ducats for three months, and Antonio bound.

BASSANIO Your answer to that? 10

SHYLOCK Antonio is a good man –

BASSANIO Have you heard any imputation to the contrary?

Shylock doubts the security of Antonio's ships, but seems willing to lend the money. He tells the audience that he hates Antonio for a variety of reasons, and intends to harm him if he can.

1 Antonio's ships

Shylock shows that he knows a lot about Antonio's business (lines 13–22). What does this knowledge suggest about Shylock's character?

2 An invitation to dinner (in pairs)

How should Shylock speak lines 27–31? Try reading these lines aloud in different ways. Talk about how you think they should be delivered. Is he joking or is he serious?

3 Shylock's hatred of Antonio (in groups)

An aside is a remark made by a character to the audience. By convention it is unheard by the other people on-stage. One of the group reads aloud Shylock's aside in lines 33–44; the others echo words which show Shylock's hatred for Antonio. Try this several times, then talk together about why Shylock hates Antonio so passionately.

4 Now it's Antonio's turn!

What would the two Christians do while Shylock makes his long aside? What if at this point Shakespeare had also written lines to the audience for Antonio to voice his feelings about Shylock? Try writing them yourself, but first look at lines 40–3, where Shylock describes Antonio's view of him and his race. Try to write Antonio's aside in the same style and rhythm as Shylock's (see page 183).

good financially sound
supposition doubt
Rialto Stock Exchange of Venice
squandered scattered
bethink me think carefully about this
to eat ... devil into to eat pig which Jesus conjured devils into from madmen's minds (see Matthew 8: 28)

publican taxman
gratis without charging interest
rate of usance rate of interest
upon the hip in a weak spot
rail criticise
thrift profit
I am ... store I'm working out how much ready cash I've got

SHYLOCK Ho no, no, no, no: my meaning in saying he is a good man
is to have you understand me that he is sufficient. Yet his means
are in supposition: he hath an argosy bound to Tripolis, another to   15
the Indies; I understand moreover upon the Rialto he hath a third
at Mexico, a fourth for England, and other ventures he hath
squandered abroad. But ships are but boards, sailors but men;
there be land rats, and water rats, water thieves and land thieves
– I mean pirates – and then there is the peril of waters, winds and   20
rocks. The man is notwithstanding sufficient. Three thousand
ducats: I think I may take his bond.

BASSANIO Be assured you may.

SHYLOCK I will be assured I may; and that I may be assured, I will
bethink me – may I speak with Antonio?   25

BASSANIO If it please you to dine with us –

SHYLOCK Yes, to smell pork, to eat of the habitation which your
prophet the Nazarite conjured the devil into. I will buy with you,
sell with you, talk with you, walk with you, and so following; but
I will not eat with you, drink with you, nor pray with you. What   30
news on the Rialto? Who is he comes here?

Enter ANTONIO

BASSANIO This is Signor Antonio.

SHYLOCK [*Aside*] How like a fawning publican he looks!
 I hate him for he is a Christian;
 But more, for that in low simplicity   35
 He lends out money gratis, and brings down
 The rate of usance here with us in Venice.
 If I can catch him once upon the hip,
 I will feed fat the ancient grudge I bear him.
 He hates our sacred nation, and he rails   40
 Even there where merchants most do congregate
 On me, my bargains, and my well-won thrift
 Which he calls interest. Cursed be my tribe
 If I forgive him!

BASSANIO   Shylock, do you hear?

SHYLOCK I am debating of my present store,   45
 And by the near guess of my memory
 I cannot instantly raise up the gross
 Of full three thousand ducats. What of that?

Shylock gently taunts Antonio for his past opposition to charging interest.
He tells a story from the Bible to show the benefits of profiting
by lending.

1 Antonio and Shylock (in pairs)

Antonio dislikes Jews and money-lending, but he has to ask Shylock
for a loan. Choose parts and read aloud lines 51–62. Pause after each
sentence to voice the secret thoughts of your character. (This is like
speaking the thought bubbles in a comic strip.)

2 Jacob and his sheep

Shylock uses a Bible story (Book of Genesis chapter 30) to justify his
way of doing business. Jacob, a descendant of Abraham, agreed to
look after his Uncle Laban's sheep. In return he could keep any
new-born lambs which were streaked or multicoloured. During the
mating season he made a fence of branches partly stripped of their
bark, so that the ewes would see the fence when they conceived (it
was believed that offspring resemble what the mother sees at
conception). As a result of Jacob's ingenuity, a large number of
streaked lambs were born, which he could keep for himself.

Can you think of another story, from the Bible or another source,
which Antonio might use to support his belief that money should be
lent for friendship and charity instead of profit? Why do you think
Shylock tells this rather involved story at this moment?

3 Bassanio and Antonio: good listeners? (in pairs)

How would Bassanio and Antonio react to Shylock's lengthy re-
telling of this Bible story? Make a tableau showing what they would
look like while they are listening.

---

in our mouths we mentioned (does
it also refer to Shylock's verbal
savaging of Antonio?)
I neither . . . excess I don't lend or
borrow for profit
ripe wants urgent needs
Is he . . . would? Does he know
how much you want?

compromised agreed
eanlings new-born lambs
hire wages
rank ready to mate
work of generation mating
And in . . . kind during mating
fulsome ewes randy sheep

        Tubal, a wealthy Hebrew of my tribe,

        Will furnish me. But soft, how many months   50

        Do you desire? [*To Antonio*] Rest you fair, good signor!

        Your worship was the last man in our mouths.

ANTONIO Shylock, albeit I neither lend nor borrow

        By taking nor by giving of excess,

        Yet to supply the ripe wants of my friend   55

        I'll break a custom. [*To Bassanio*] Is he yet possessed

        How much ye would?

SHYLOCK   Ay, ay, three thousand ducats.

ANTONIO And for three months.

SHYLOCK I had forgot, three months; [*To Bassanio*] you told me so.

        Well then, your bond; and let me see – but hear you,   60

        Methoughts you said you neither lend nor borrow

        Upon advantage.

ANTONIO   I do never use it.

SHYLOCK When Jacob grazed his uncle Laban's sheep –

        This Jacob from our holy Abram was

        (As his wise mother wrought in his behalf)   65

        The third possessor; ay, he was the third –

ANTONIO And what of him, did he take interest?

SHYLOCK No, not take interest, not as you would say

        Directly interest. Mark what Jacob did:

        When Laban and himself were compromised   70

        That all the eanlings which were streaked and pied

        Should fall as Jacob's hire, the ewes being rank

        In end of autumn turnèd to the rams,

        And when the work of generation was

        Between these woolly breeders in the act,   75

        The skilful shepherd pilled me certain wands

        And in the doing of the deed of kind

        He stuck them up before the fulsome ewes,

        Who then conceiving, did in eaning time

        Fall parti-coloured lambs, and those were Jacob's.   80

        This was a way to thrive, and he was blest;

        And thrift is blessing if men steal it not.

Antonio is not convinced by Shylock's argument. He warns Bassanio not to be deceived by the Jew's use of the Bible. Shylock reminds Antonio of the contemptuous way he has been treated in the past.

1 Antonio's warning (in small groups)

Antonio interrupts Shylock (line 89) to warn Bassanio against Bible-quoting villains.

Read Antonio's advice to his friend (lines 89–94). Decide whether Antonio intends Shylock to hear what is said. Is 'the devil' meant to be Shylock, or Lucifer himself?

Antonio uses vivid images. Choose one of his lines and show it as a mime to the rest of the class. Can they recognise which one you have chosen?

2 Smiling villains (line 92)

Shakespeare often used the image of the smiling villain:

'There's daggers in men's smiles' (*Macbeth*)
'One may smile and smile and be a villain' (*Hamlet*)
'Why, I can smile, and murder whiles I smile' (*Richard III*).

Write a poem or short story entitled 'A villain with a smiling cheek'.

3 Shylock versus Antonio (in pairs)

Take turns to speak and perform Shylock's lines 98–121 to each other. Experiment with different tones of voice, gestures and the positioning of the two enemies. Emphasise key words and phrases. In one production, Shylock stood face to face with Antonio. In another, Shylock lay relaxed on cushions and spoke in a half-amused tone. In yet another, Shylock sneered at and mocked Antonio as he circled him. Work out what you think is the most appropriate staging.

This was . . . heaven God was responsible for Jacob's good luck
inserted mentioned
holy witness evidence from the Bible
beholding indebted

rated insulted
gaberdine coat
void your rheum spit
stranger cur stray dog
bondman's key slave's voice

ANTONIO This was a venture, sir, that Jacob served for,
   A thing not in his power to bring to pass,
   But swayed and fashioned by the hand of heaven. 85
   Was this inserted to make interest good?
   Or is your gold and silver ewes and rams?
SHYLOCK I cannot tell, I make it breed as fast.
   But note me, signor –
ANTONIO   Mark you this, Bassanio,
   The devil can cite Scripture for his purpose. 90
   An evil soul producing holy witness
   Is like a villain with a smiling cheek,
   A goodly apple rotten at the heart.
   O what a goodly outside falsehood hath!
SHYLOCK Three thousand ducats, 'tis a good round sum. 95
   Three months from twelve, then let me see, the rate –
ANTONIO Well, Shylock, shall we be beholding to you?
SHYLOCK Signor Antonio, many a time and oft
   In the Rialto you have rated me
   About my monies and my usances. 100
   Still have I borne it with a patient shrug
   For suff'rance is the badge of all our tribe.
   You call me misbeliever, cut-throat dog,
   And spit upon my Jewish gaberdine,
   And all for use of that which is mine own. 105
   Well then, it now appears you need my help.
   Go to, then, you come to me, and you say,
   'Shylock, we would have monies' – you say so,
   You that did void your rheum upon my beard,
   And foot me as you spurn a stranger cur 110
   Over your threshold: monies is your suit.
   What should I say to you? Should I not say
   'Hath a dog money? Is it possible
   A cur can lend three thousand ducats?' Or
   Shall I bend low, and in a bondman's key, 115
   With bated breath and whisp'ring humbleness,
   Say this:
   'Fair sir, you spat on me on Wednesday last,
   You spurned me such a day, another time
   You called me dog: and for these courtesies 120
   I'll lend you thus much monies.'

Antonio remains contemptuous, but Shylock claims to want his friendship, offering not to charge interest on the loan. Instead, if Antonio fails to pay, Shylock will take a pound of his flesh.

1 Making money from money

Antonio shows his disdain for charging interest by describing it as 'A breed for barren metal' (making money from money). But is there anything wrong with charging interest?

Collect examples from newspapers of modern practices of paying interest on loans. Find out the difference between 'interest' and 'usury'.

2 An argument avoided (in pairs)

Take parts and read lines 122–35. Imagine you are directing the play. Write notes for the actors about how they could speak these lines for dramatic effect. How angry (if at all) should Antonio be? How and why has Shylock's tone changed from that of his earlier language?

3 The 'single bond'

Shylock proposes 'a merry sport': if Antonio cannot repay the loan, he must forfeit a pound of his flesh.

Imagine you are the notary. Write your own version of the bond between Shylock and Antonio. This bond is a formal business document, so use appropriate language. Include all the agreed terms of the loan, and add the signatures of both parties and witnesses.

4 The Christians' 'hard dealings' (in pairs)

Talk together about what Shylock has in mind when he talks of Christian behaviour (lines 153–5), then make up a soundtrack of some of the things the Christians might have said to Shylock in the past. You could tape-record these or speak them 'live' to the rest of the class to show the 'hard dealings' of the Christians.

---

take . . . friend make money from lending to a friend
break goes bankrupt
no doit of usance not one penny of interest
notary lawyer

in a merry sport just for a joke
I'll . . . necessity I'd rather stay in debt
exaction . . . forfeiture demanding the forfeit (the pound of flesh)

ANTONIO I am as like to call thee so again,
    To spit on thee again, to spurn thee too.
    If thou wilt lend this money, lend it not
    As to thy friends, for when did friendship take   125
    A breed for barren metal of his friend?
    But lend it rather to thine enemy,
    Who if he break, thou mayst with better face
    Exact the penalty.
SHYLOCK Why look you how you storm!   130
    I would be friends with you, and have your love,
    Forget the shames that you have stained me with,
    Supply your present wants, and take no doit
    Of usance for my monies, and you'll not hear me.
    This is kind I offer.
BASSANIO   This were kindness.   135
SHYLOCK This kindness will I show.
    Go with me to a notary, seal me there
    Your single bond, and, in a merry sport,
    If you repay me not on such a day,
    In such a place, such sum or sums as are   140
    Expressed in the condition, let the forfeit
    Be nominated for an equal pound
    Of your fair flesh, to be cut off and taken
    In what part of your body pleaseth me.
ANTONIO Content, in faith! I'll seal to such a bond,   145
    And say there is much kindness in the Jew.
BASSANIO You shall not seal to such a bond for me;
    I'll rather dwell in my necessity.
ANTONIO Why, fear not, man, I will not forfeit it.
    Within these two months, that's a month before   150
    This bond expires, I do expect return
    Of thrice three times the value of this bond.
SHYLOCK O father Abram, what these Christians are,
    Whose own hard dealings teaches them suspect
    The thoughts of others! Pray you tell me this: 155
    If he should break his day what should I gain
    By the exaction of the forfeiture?

Shylock insists that he can gain nothing from the deal except Antonio's friendship. Antonio agrees to the terms, and Shylock leaves to fetch the money. Bassanio is still uneasy about the contract.

1 'A pound of man's flesh' (in pairs)

Share your reactions to Shylock's estimation of the value of human flesh (lines 158–60). What might his motives be in saying this?

2 In the lawyer's chambers (in groups of four)

Improvise the visit of Bassanio, Antonio and Shylock to the notary's. How would the lawyer react to the extraordinary terms of the bond?

3 The last lines

The last four lines (171–4) are rhyming couplets (they rhyme in pairs). Write your own rhyming couplet as two exit lines for Shylock in which he comments on the bond.

Look closely at this 1932 set design for the Rialto. It can be either the Stock Exchange or a bridge, depending on the director's intentions. Talk about what this set suggests about life in Venice. How does it fit in with the ideas you have so far developed about the city as presented in the play?

---

muttons, beefs sheep and cattle
adieu goodbye

unthrifty knave careless servant
presently immediately

A pound of man's flesh, taken from a man,
Is not so estimable, profitable neither,
As flesh of muttons, beefs, or goats. I say   160
To buy his favour, I extend this friendship.
If he will take it, so; if not, adieu,
And for my love, I pray you wrong me not.
ANTONIO Yes, Shylock, I will seal unto this bond.
SHYLOCK Then meet me forthwith at the notary's.   165
    Give him direction for this merry bond,
    And I will go and purse the ducats straight,
    See to my house left in the fearful guard
    Of an unthrifty knave, and presently
    I'll be with you.   *Exit*
ANTONIO   Hie thee, gentle Jew.   170
    The Hebrew will turn Christian, he grows kind.   *mocking*
BASSANIO I like not fair terms and a villain's mind.   *religion*
ANTONIO Come on, in this there can be no dismay,
    My ships come home a month before the day.

Exeunt

Looking back at Act 1
Activities for groups or individuals

1 What kind of a city is Venice?

Write your impressions of what life is like in Shylock's Venice. Think about such matters as religion, class, occupations, attitudes to race, and the roles of men and women.

2 Antonio: a case study

What do you make of Antonio? He is obviously popular with his friends and has a close relationship with Bassanio, but he has been cruel to Shylock. He is also depressed, though there is no clear explanation for his sadness. Imagine you are a psychiatrist. Write a case study of Antonio based on his language, his behaviour, and what others have said about him in Act 1.

3 Belmont: what's it like?

Design a stage set to show your image of Belmont. Think about how you would portray Portia's wealth and her marriage predicament.

4 Shylock's religion

Collect from Scene 3 references to Shylock's religious beliefs. Talk together about how his religion affects his behaviour and attitudes.

5 Continuing conversations

At the start of all three scenes in Act 1 the characters enter already deep in conversation. Talk together about why you think Shakespeare introduces his characters in this way. Discuss each scene opening.

6 Portia's father

All we know about Portia's father is that he was rich, he probably died after his wife (there is no mention of Portia's mother), and he left his daughter at the mercy of a lucky dip! Think about his possible reasons for leaving his only child in such a difficult situation. What if there was an explanatory letter to accompany the will? As Portia's father, write your own version of the letter.

7 Fathers and daughters

Find which other Shakespeare plays feature problems between fathers and daughters (see page 72). There are quite a few of them! Shakespeare had two daughters himself (see page 188). Research Shakespeare's family history to discover if there is any evidence of bad feeling between him and his own daughters.

8 The bond and the quest

Now that Antonio has signed the bond, Bassanio knows that he has the money to pursue his quest to win the wealthy Portia. Make up an extra scene in which Bassanio tells his friend Lorenzo of his doubts about the contract with Shylock and his hopes concerning his forthcoming visit to Belmont. Has he already heard about the caskets? Perhaps Lorenzo tells him about them.

9 Portrait gallery

Choose one character from Act 1. Invent a typical gesture or movement for her or him. Show the rest of the class. Can they guess your character?

10 Favourite lines

Look back through the act and choose the three or four lines that appeal to you most. Learn them by heart and work out a way of presenting them to the rest of the class.

11 Shylock: how much is 'aside'?

No one knows for certain which lines Shakespeare intended to be spoken directly to the audience as 'asides'. Over the centuries, editors of the plays have made their own judgements about which lines are 'asides' and which are not, and in every production, actors take similar (and often different) decisions. Imagine you are playing Shylock. Look through Scene 3 and decide which of his lines you would speak as asides. Give reasons for your choice.

12 Cast the play

You are a director about to film the play. Who would you choose for your actors? Choose anyone you think suitable: public figures, film or rock or sports stars, your teachers or classmates . . . the choice is yours! Say why you have cast particular people in particular roles . . .

*The Prince of Morocco arrives to try to win Portia's hand in marriage.
Portia stresses that she must obey her dead father's will and marry the man
who solves the riddle of the caskets.*

1 Enter Morocco (in groups of ten or twelve)

Morocco has come to Belmont to seek Portia's hand in marriage. He
wants to create an impression of his eminence and importance. Study
the stage direction at the beginning of the scene, then act out the
entrance of the two groups of characters. Highlight the sense of
ceremony. Add sound or music as appropriate.

2 Morocco: serious or comic or . . .? (in pairs)

Every production has to decide just how to present Morocco. Is he
noble and dignified, or a comic windbag, or . . .? Make up your own
mind through the following activities. Take it in turns to read aloud
Morocco's two speeches (lines 1–12 and lines 22–38).

- Through voice and gesture, make them exaggerated and funny.
- Make them sensational and melodramatic.
- Read them as seriously as you can, to show him as genuinely noble.
- From Morocco's second speech (lines 22–38) choose one brave
  deed that he refers to, and mime it. Show your work to another
  pair. Can they guess which deed you chose?

3 Portia's inner conflict (in pairs)

Take turns to read aloud Portia's speech (lines 13–22). Although she
is being polite to Morocco, what do you think she really feels about
the possibility of being married to him? Try reading the speech again
to bring out the tension between her duty to her dead father's will and
her feelings towards Morocco.

---

shadowed livery dark uniform
burnished brightly polished
Phoebus the sun god
feared terrified
clime climate
nice over-fussy

scanted restricted
hedged limited
scimitar sword with a curved blade
Sophy Shah of Persia
fields battles
a roars he roars

ACT 2   SCENE 1
Belmont   A room in Portia's house

A flourish of cornets. Enter the Prince of MOROCCO, *a tawny Moor all in white, and three or four followers accordingly; with* PORTIA, NERISSA, *and their train*

MOROCCO Mislike me not for my complexion,
          The shadowed livery of the burnished sun,
          To whom I am a neighbour and near bred.
          Bring me the fairest creature northward born,
          Where Phoebus' fire scarce thaws the icicles,   5
          And let us make incision for your love
          To prove whose blood is reddest, his or mine.
          I tell thee, lady, this aspèct of mine
          Hath feared the valiant; by my love I swear
          The best-regarded virgins of our clime   10
          Have loved it too. I would not change this hue,
          Except to steal your thoughts, my gentle queen.
PORTIA In terms of choice I am not solely led
          By nice direction of a maiden's eyes.
          Besides, the lottery of my destiny   15
          Bars me the right of voluntary choosing.
          But if my father had not scanted me,
          And hedged me by his wit to yield myself
          His wife who wins me by that means I told you,
          Yourself, renownèd prince, then stood as fair   20
          As any comer I have looked on yet
          For my affection.
MOROCCO   Even for that I thank you.
          Therefore I pray you lead me to the caskets
          To try my fortune. By this scimitar,
          That slew the Sophy and a Persian prince   25
          That won three fields of Sultan Solyman,
          I would o'er-stare the sternest eyes that look,
          Outbrave the heart most daring on the earth,
          Pluck the young sucking cubs from the she-bear,
          Yea, mock the lion when a roars for prey,   30

Portia reminds Morocco that he must swear an oath and, after dinner, is to make his choice of casket. Scene 2 introduces Lancelot Gobbo, Shylock's servant, who is considering deserting his master.

1 Our second look at Portia (in groups of three or four)

This is the second scene to feature Portia: she appeared before in Act 1 Scene 2. Read quickly through what she says in both scenes, then make a list of any ways in which Portia's mood is consistent.

2 'Forward to the temple' (in pairs)

At 'the temple' (Belmont's church) Morocco must swear an oath never to marry if he chooses the wrong casket. On their way to the oath ceremony, Nerissa and Portia could have a private conversation about their impressions of Morocco. What would they say about him? Improvise their talk.

3 What's in a name? (in pairs)

Before you read Scene 2, talk about the impressions created by the name Lancelot Gobbo. What does it suggest to you about his character and personality?

4 Lancelot struggles with his conscience
(in groups of three)

Read aloud Lancelot's speech (lines 1–24). One person plays Lancelot Gobbo, another his 'conscience' and the third 'the fiend' who is tempting him. Add actions and gestures to emphasise the debate that seems to be taking place in Lancelot's mind. In the light of this experience, what advice would you give to an actor about performing this speech?

Hercules and Lichas a legendary Greek hero and his servant
Alcides another name for Hercules
hazard gamble
will serve me will permit me

the fiend devil
pack be gone
did something smack was like that (or kissed noisily)

To win thee, lady. But alas the while,
If Hercules and Lichas play at dice
Which is the better man, the greater throw
May turn by fortune from the weaker hand.
So is Alcides beaten by his rage,   35
And so may I, blind Fortune leading me,
Miss that which one unworthier may attain,
And die with grieving.

PORTIA   You must take your chance,
And either not attempt to choose at all
Or swear before you choose, if you choose wrong,   40
Never to speak to lady afterward
In way of marriage: therefore be advised.

MOROCCO Nor will not. Come, bring me unto my chance.

PORTIA First forward to the temple; after dinner
Your hazard shall be made.

MOROCCO   Good fortune then,   45
To make me blest – or cursèd'st among men!

Cornets. Exeunt

ACT 2   SCENE 2
Venice   Near Shylock's house

Enter LANCELOT GOBBO, *the Clown, alone*

LANCELOT Certainly, my conscience will serve me to run from this Jew
my master. The fiend is at mine elbow and tempts me, saying to me
'Gobbo, Lancelot Gobbo, good Lancelot', or 'Good Gobbo', or
'Good Lancelot Gobbo, use your legs, take the start, run away.'
My conscience says 'No: take heed, honest Lancelot, take heed,   5
honest Gobbo' – or (as aforesaid) – 'honest Lancelot Gobbo; do
not run, scorn running with thy heels.' Well, the most courageous
fiend bids me pack. 'Fia!' says the fiend, 'Away!' says the fiend.
''Fore the heavens, rouse up a brave mind', says the fiend, 'and
run.' Well, my conscience, hanging about the neck of my heart,   10
says very wisely to me, 'My honest friend Lancelot, being an honest
man's son, or rather an honest woman's son' (for indeed my
father did something smack, something grow to; he had a kind of
taste): well, my conscience says 'Lancelot, budge not!' 'Budge!'

Lancelot Gobbo resolves to leave Shylock's service. Lancelot's nearly blind father arrives, looking for Lancelot, but does not recognise his son. Lancelot decides to play a trick on him.

1 Down and out in Venice?

What impression does this picture of Lancelot and his father create of the life of working-class people in Venice? How does it contrast with what you have so far seen of Venice and Belmont?

2 'I will try confusions with him' (in pairs)

Read the exchange between Lancelot and his father (lines 25–53).

Does Lancelot disguise his voice to deceive Gobbo? Talk together about Lancelot's treatment of his blind father. Is it humorous, or merely cruel?

Improvise an argument between someone who likes this part of the scene and someone who disapproves of it as being in bad taste and not relevant.

---

incarnation Lancelot means 'incarnate' ('made flesh')
sand-blind half-blind
gravel-blind nearly totally blind
Marry by St Mary
be God's sonties by God's saints

raise the waters make him cry
a will he will
ergo therefore
sisters three the three Fates who decide human destiny

says the fiend.'Budge not!' says my conscience. 'Conscience', say   15
I, 'you counsel well.' 'Fiend', say I, 'you counsel well.' To be
ruled by my conscience, I should stay with the Jew my master
who – God bless the mark! – is a kind of devil; and to run away
from the Jew, I should be ruled by the fiend who – saving your
reverence – is the devil himself. Certainly the Jew is the very devil   20
incarnation, and, in my conscience, my conscience is but a kind of
hard conscience to offer to counsel me to stay with the Jew. The
fiend gives the more friendly counsel: I will run, fiend, my heels
are at your commandment, I will run.

Enter OLD GOBBO *with a basket*

GOBBO Master young-man, you, I pray you, which is the way to Master   25
Jew's?

LANCELOT [*Aside*] O heavens! This is my true-begotten father who
being more than sand-blind, high gravel-blind, knows me not. I
will try confusions with him.

GOBBO Master young-gentleman, I pray you, which is the way to   30
Master Jew's?

LANCELOT Turn upon your right hand at the next turning, but at the
next turning of all on your left. Marry, at the very next turning
turn of no hand but turn down indirectly to the Jew's house.

GOBBO Be God's sonties, 'twill be a hard way to hit! Can you tell me   35
whether one Lancelot that dwells with him, dwell with him or
no?

LANCELOT Talk you of young Master Lancelot? [*Aside*] Mark me now,
now will I raise the waters. Talk you of young Master Lancelot?

GOBBO No 'master', sir, but a poor man's son. His father, though I   40
say't, is an honest, exceeding poor man and, God be thanked, well
to live.

LANCELOT Well, let his father be what a will, we talk of young Master
Lancelot.

GOBBO Your worship's friend and Lancelot, sir.   45

LANCELOT But I pray you, *ergo* old man, *ergo* I beseech you, talk you
of young Master Lancelot?

GOBBO Of Lancelot, an't please your mastership.

LANCELOT *Ergo* Master Lancelot. Talk not of Master Lancelot, father,
for the young gentleman, according to fates and destinies, and such   50
odd sayings, the sisters three, and such branches of learning, is
indeed deceased, or as you would say in plain terms, gone to
heaven.

After several attempts, Lancelot convinces his father that he is indeed talking to his own son. Lancelot plans to enter the service of Bassanio.

---

1 Stage business (in pairs)

Actors often invent stage 'business' (actions, gestures) to help modern audiences understand language and jokes which are no longer clear. There are some expressions opposite with which a modern audience often needs help. Work out what 'business' could be added to the following to bring out their humour:

- 'Do I look like a cudgel or a hovel-post, a staff or a prop?' (line 56)
- 'Thou has got more hair on thy chin than Dobbin my fill-horse has on his tail' (lines 77–8).
- 'I have brought him a present' (line 83).
- 'You may tell every finger I have with my ribs' (lines 87–8).

Show your ideas to the rest of the class.

2 A letter from Lancelot

As Lancelot, imagine that you wrote to your father just after entering Shylock's service. Look at lines 85–92 for clues to what you might report. Add extra details as appropriate, then write the letter.

3 Prejudice at all levels? (in groups of three or four)

'For I am a Jew if I serve the Jew any longer'.

Talk together about what Lancelot's remark tells you about the attitude of the poor people of Venice towards the Jews.

---

staff of my age support in my old age
hovel-post post to hold up a shelter

fill-horse carthorse
set up my rest determined
halter noose to hang himself
liveries uniforms

GOBBO Marry, God forbid! The boy was the very staff of my age, my
  very prop.   55
LANCELOT Do I look like a cudgel or a hovel-post, a staff or a prop?
  Do you know me, father?
GOBBO Alack the day, I know you not, young gentleman, but I pray
  you tell me, is my boy – God rest his soul! – alive or dead?
LANCELOT Do you not know me, father?   60
GOBBO Alack, sir, I am sand-blind, I know you not.
LANCELOT Nay indeed, if you had your eyes you might fail of the
  knowing me: it is a wise father that knows his own child. Well, old
  man, I will tell you news of your son. [*Kneels*] Give me your
  blessing; truth will come to light, murder cannot be hid long, a   65
  man's son may, but in the end truth will out.
GOBBO Pray you, sir, stand up; I am sure you are not Lancelot my
  boy.
LANCELOT Pray you, let's have no more fooling about it, but give me
  your blessing; I am Lancelot your boy that was, your son that is,   70
  your child that shall be.
GOBBO I cannot think you are my son.
LANCELOT I know not what I shall think of that; but I am Lancelot the
  Jew's man, and I am sure Margery your wife is my mother.
GOBBO Her name is Margery indeed. I'll be sworn if thou be Lancelot   75
  thou art mine own flesh and blood. Lord worshipped might he be,
  what a beard hast thou got! Thou has got more hair on thy chin
  than Dobbin my fill-horse has on his tail.
LANCELOT It should seem then that Dobbin's tail grows backward. I
  am sure he had more hair of his tail than I have of my face when   80
  I last saw him.
GOBBO Lord, how art thou changed! How dost thou and thy master
  agree? I have brought him a present. How 'gree you now?
LANCELOT Well, well; but for mine own part, as I have set up my rest
  to run away, so I will not rest till I have run some ground. My   85
  master's a very Jew. Give him a present? Give him a halter! I am
  famished in his service; you may tell every finger I have with my
  ribs. Father, I am glad you are come; give me your present to one
  Master Bassanio, who indeed gives rare new liveries: if I serve not
  him, I will run as far as God has any ground. O rare fortune, here   90
  comes the man! To him, father, for I am a Jew if I serve the Jew
  any longer.

Bassanio sends a servant to fetch Gratiano. Lancelot and his father try to persuade Bassanio to employ Lancelot. Bassanio says that Shylock has already recommended Lancelot to him.

1 Two people trying to tell the same story (in pairs)

Take parts and read aloud Lancelot and Gobbo's lines 97–115 so that each speech follows on quickly from the other. Stress the comedy and confusion that arise when two characters compete in telling the same story, trying to speak almost at the same time.

2 Malapropisms (in groups of three or four)

A malapropism is 'a comical confusion of words', usually when a person chooses the wrong word in mistake for another that sounds like it. Gobbo uses several between lines 103 and 118. Find them and talk about the words he really meant to use. Make up some sentences of your own that include malapropisms.

(Malapropisms are named after Mrs Malaprop, who muddled up her language in Sheridan's play *The Rivals*. Shakespeare would have known malapropisms as 'cacozelia'.)

3 'Shylock thy master spoke with me this day' (in pairs)

Bassanio tells us that he has already spoken to Shylock about the possibility of employing Lancelot Gobbo. What else might they have said? Improvise the conversation.

4 Prose and verse (in pairs)

Bassanio (lines 119–23) changes from speaking prose to verse. Talk together about the effects of this change in language style. Can you give three or four possible reasons why Shakespeare makes the change here?

---

anon at once
Gramercy God have mercy
aught anything
scarce cater-cousins hardly close
 friends
preferred recommended

the old proverb 'The grace of God
 is gear enough' (God's grace is
 sufficient)
parted divided
enough wealth

Enter BASSANIO *with* [LEONARDO *and*] *a follower or two*

BASSANIO You may do so, but let it be so hasted that supper be ready
at the farthest by five of the clock. See these letters delivered, put
the liveries to making, and desire Gratiano to come anon to my   95
lodging.

[Exit one of his men]

LANCELOT To him, father.

GOBBO God bless your worship!

BASSANIO Gramercy; wouldst thou aught with me?

GOBBO Here's my son, sir, a poor boy –   100

LANCELOT Not a poor boy, sir, but the rich Jew's man that would, sir,
as my father shall specify –

GOBBO He hath a great infection, sir, as one would say, to serve –

LANCELOT Indeed, the short and the long is, I serve the Jew, and have
a desire, as my father shall specify –   105

GOBBO His master and he, saving your worship's reverence, are scarce
cater-cousins –

LANCELOT To be brief, the very truth is that the Jew having done me
wrong doth cause me – as my father being I hope an old man shall
frutify unto you –   110

GOBBO I have here a dish of doves that I would bestow upon your
worship, and my suit is –

LANCELOT In very brief, the suit is impertinent to myself, as your
worship shall know by this honest old man, and though I say it,
though old man, yet poor man, my father –   115

BASSANIO One speak for both. What would you?

LANCELOT Serve you, sir.

GOBBO That is the very defect of the matter, sir.

BASSANIO I know thee well, thou hast obtained thy suit.

       Shylock thy master spoke with me this day,   120

       And hath preferred thee, if it be preferment

       To leave a rich Jew's service to become

       The follower of so poor a gentleman.

LANCELOT The old proverb is very well parted between my master
Shylock and you, sir: you have the grace of God, sir, and he hath   125
enough.

Lancelot welcomes the prospect of serving Bassanio, who plans to entertain Antonio that night. Gratiano wishes to travel with Bassanio to Belmont. Bassanio advises him to improve his rough manners.

1 'Give him a livery'

From now on, Lancelot will belong to Bassanio's household. Design a costume for Lancelot to wear as Bassanio's servant.

2 Lancelot the fortune-teller (in pairs)

Lancelot fancies himself as a fortune-teller as he reads his own palm. If he had the chance to read the palms of some of the other characters, what might he foretell? One person plays Lancelot, the other chooses to be:

Shylock or
Antonio or
Bassanio or
Portia.

Take it in turns to be Lancelot and the person having her/his fortune told. Base your predictions on what you know of the play so far.

3 'These things being bought and orderly bestowed'

Bassanio is preparing for the trip to Belmont. If you were Bassanio, what would you take with you on the ship? Think carefully about why he is actually going to Belmont, then prepare your list.

4 Bassanio's fears about Gratiano
   (in groups of three or four)

Read Bassanio's lines 151–60 to each other. He expresses concern that Gratiano's wild behaviour will spoil his courtship of Portia. Emphasise key words, then improvise one example of Gratiano's past behaviour that has prompted Bassanio's concern.

---

guarded elaborate
fairer table luckier palm
coming-in beginning
'scape escape
'scapes adventures
gear matter

best esteemed acquaintance best
  friend
suit a favour to ask
parts characteristics
liberal free, licentious, over-the-top
misconstered misinterpreted

BASSANIO Thou speak'st it well; go, father, with thy son;
       Take leave of thy old master, and enquire
       My lodging out. [*To a follower*] Give him a livery
       More guarded than his fellows'; see it done.   130
LANCELOT Father, in. I cannot get a service, no, I have ne'er a tongue
in my head! [*Looks at palm of his hand*] Well, if any man in Italy
have a fairer table which doth offer to swear upon a book! – I shall
have good fortune. Go to, here's a simple line of life, here's a
small trifle of wives: alas, fifteen wives is nothing, eleven widows   135
and nine maids is a simple coming-in for one man. And then to
'scape drowning thrice, and to be in peril of my life with the edge
of a featherbed: here are simple 'scapes. Well, if Fortune be a
woman, she's a good wench for this gear. Father, come, I'll take my
leave of the Jew in the twinkling.   140
                        Exeunt Lancelot [and Gobbo]
BASSANIO I pray thee, good Leonardo, think on this.
       These things being bought and orderly bestowed,
       Return in haste, for I do feast tonight
       My best esteemed acquaintance. Hie thee, go.
LEONARDO My best endeavours shall be done herein.   145

             Enter GRATIANO

GRATIANO Where's your master?
LEONARDO   Yonder, sir, he walks.   *Exit*
GRATIANO Signor Bassanio!
BASSANIO Gratiano?
GRATIANO I have a suit to you.
BASSANIO   You have obtained it.
GRATIANO You must not deny me, I must go with you to Belmont.   150
BASSANIO Why then, you must. But hear thee, Gratiano:
       Thou art too wild, too rude, and bold of voice –
       Parts that become thee happily enough,
       And in such eyes as ours appear not faults;
       But where thou art not known, why there they show   155
       Something too liberal. Pray thee take pain
       To allay with some cold drops of modesty
       Thy skipping spirit, lest through thy wild behaviour
       I be misconstered in the place I go to,
       And lose my hopes.

Gratiano promises to behave respectably in Belmont – but not tonight!
In Scene 3, Jessica laments Lancelot's imminent departure. She hands him
a letter to give secretly to Lorenzo.

1 'Put on a sober habit' (in pairs)

Once again, Gratiano talks about playing a part: in lines 160–8 he promises to behave himself. Remember he has already offered to 'play the fool' for Antonio.

Choose one of Gratiano's examples of polite behaviour. Mime it. Can your partner guess which one you have chosen?

Talk about the occasions in real life when you find yourself playing a part (at school, with your family, at work, with friends, etc.). Think carefully about the different ways you speak in different situations. Work out a series of brief improvisations based on the ideas which come out of your discussion.

Does Gratiano seem the kind of person who will keep his word to behave?

2 Jessica's home life (in groups of three or four)

Jessica seems very unhappy at home: 'Our house is hell'.
Read all Jessica says in this scene, then:

- Devise a series of three tableaux which you think capture some of the reasons for her unhappiness.

- As Jessica, each person writes a letter to the problem page of a teenage magazine. Describe the problems you have at home, and ask if you are right to desert your father for Lorenzo and convert to Christianity. Read each other's letters and make up suitable replies.

---

a sober habit serious behaviour
hood cover
civility manners
studied practised
ostent appearance
bar except
gauge judge

suit of mirth cheerful mood
ducat gold coin
exhibit inhibit (he chooses the
  wrong word)
pagan someone who is not a
  Christian

GRATIANO   Signor Bassanio, hear me: 160
         If I do not put on a sober habit,
         Talk with respect, and swear but now and then,
         Wear prayer books in my pocket, look demurely,
         Nay more, while grace is saying, hood mine eyes
         Thus with my hat, and sigh and say 'amen',   165
         Use all the observance of civility
         Like one well studied in a sad ostent
         To please his grandam, never trust me more.
BASSANIO Well, we shall see your bearing.
GRATIANO Nay, but I bar tonight, you shall not gauge me   170
         By what we do tonight.
BASSANIO   No, that were pity.
         I would entreat you rather to put on
         Your boldest suit of mirth, for we have friends
         That purpose merriment. But fare you well,
         I have some business.   175
GRATIANO And I must to Lorenzo and the rest;
         But we will visit you at supper time.   *Exeunt*

ACT 2   SCENE 3
Venice

Enter JESSICA and LANCELOT the Clown

JESSICA I am sorry thou wilt leave my father so.
         Our house is hell, and thou a merry devil
         Didst rob it of some taste of tediousness.
         But fare thee well: there is a ducat for thee.
         And, Lancelot, soon at supper shalt thou see   5
         Lorenzo, who is thy new master's guest;
         Give him this letter, do it secretly.
         And so farewell: I would not have my father
         See me in talk with thee.
LANCELOT Adieu; tears exhibit my tongue. Most beautiful pagan,   10
         most sweet Jew, if a Christian do not play the knave and get thee,
         I am much deceived. But adieu; these foolish drops do something
         drown my manly spirit. Adieu!   [*Exit*]

*Jessica, ashamed to be Shylock's daughter, plans to marry Lorenzo
and become a Christian. In Scene 4, arrangements for a masque are made.
Lancelot delivers Jessica's letter.*

1 Jessica's exit (in pairs)

One person plays Jessica, the other is the director. Think about
Jessica's state of mind as she says her lines. Work out how she exits
from this scene, concentrating on the exact impression you wish to
create for an audience. Freeze the sequence at a telling point. Show
your work to other groups.

2 'Disguise us' (in groups of four)

The four men plan to attend a masque (an entertainment with music,
torches, dancing and elaborate masks and disguises). They must all
wear disguises, as was the custom. The disguise might be a mask, a
costume, or both. There is a very similar scene of young men
preparing for a masque in *Romeo and Juliet* Act 1 Scene 4. Choose
one character each and produce a disguise which reflects his
personality. Display your ideas.

3 Directing the scene (in groups of five)

Take parts and read Scene 4 aloud. Then, as if you are directing the
play, write a series of detailed notes to the characters, explaining how
you think this scene should be played. Look out for clues about the
time of day and the characters' changing moods. How will you handle
the various entrances and exits?

4 'Hold here, take this' (in pairs)

'This' in line 19 might be a tip for Lancelot, the go-between, or it
could be a gift for Jessica. Talk about this kind of gift Lorenzo might
want to send to Jessica. Give reasons for your choice.

---

heinous dreadful
strife divided feelings (duty and
  love)
quaintly ordered carefully
  organised

break up unseal
hand handwriting

JESSICA Farewell, good Lancelot.
        Alack, what heinous sin is it in me   15
        To be ashamed to be my father's child!
        But though I am a daughter to his blood
        I am not to his manners. O Lorenzo,
        If thou keep promise, I shall end this strife,
        Become a Christian and thy loving wife.   *Exit*   20

ACT 2   SCENE 4
Venice

Enter GRATIANO, LORENZO, SALARINO, *and* SOLANIO

LORENZO Nay, we will slink away in supper time,
        Disguise us at my lodging, and return
        All in an hour.
GRATIANO We have not made good preparation.
SALARINO We have not spoke us yet of torchbearers.   5
SOLANIO 'Tis vile unless it may be quaintly ordered,
        And better in my mind not undertook.
LORENZO 'Tis now but four of clock; we have two hours
        To furnish us.

Enter LANCELOT [*with a letter*]

                    Friend Lancelot! What's the news?
LANCELOT And it shall please you to break up this, it shall seem to   10
    signify.
LORENZO I know the hand; in faith, 'tis a fair hand,
        And whiter than the paper it writ on
        Is the fair hand that writ.
GRATIANO   Love news, in faith!
LANCELOT By your leave, sir.   15
LORENZO Whither goest thou?
LANCELOT Marry, sir, to bid my old master the Jew to sup tonight
    with my new master the Christian.
LORENZO Hold here, take this. Tell gentle Jessica
        I will not fail her; speak it privately.   20
                                    Exit Lancelot

Lorenzo tells Gratiano that Jessica plans to disguise herself as a boy and flee from Shylock, taking some of his gold and jewels. Scene 5 begins with Shylock talking of his generosity to Lancelot.

1 'That letter from fair Jessica' (in pairs)

Read Lorenzo's lines 29–39 aloud to each other. Use the information to write your version of Jessica's letter to Lorenzo.

- Read aloud, or tape-record, your letter.
- One partner reads the letter aloud, the other gives Lorenzo's reactions to what Jessica has written.

2 Shylock at home (in groups of three)

Scene 5 gives a glimpse of Shylock's home life and his relationship to Jessica. To gain a first impression, take parts as Shylock, Lancelot and Jessica, and quickly read through the scene.

3 'The difference of old Shylock and Bassanio' (in groups of three or four)

What differences have you noticed between the two men Shylock and Bassanio, and their households? Make a list of the points that emerge.

4 'What, Jessica!' (in pairs)

Read Shylock's lines 1–6 aloud to each other. He is talking directly to Lancelot and trying to summon Jessica to him at the same time. As you read, stress Shylock's growing impatience.

---

page a young male servant
foot path
issue child
faithless lacking the Christian faith

gourmandise over-eat
rend apparel out wear clothes out
 by tearing them
was wont to tell often told

Go, gentlemen:
Will you prepare you for this masque tonight?
I am provided of a torchbearer.
SALARINO Ay marry, I'll be gone about it straight.
SOLANIO And so will I.
LORENZO   Meet me and Gratiano   25
        At Gratiano's lodging some hour hence.
SALARINO 'Tis good we do so.

Exeunt [Salarino and Solanio]

GRATIANO Was not that letter from fair Jessica?
LORENZO I must needs tell thee all. She hath directed
        How I shall take her from her father's house,   30
        What gold and jewels she is furnished with,
        What page's suit she hath in readiness.
        If e'er the Jew her father come to heaven,
        It will be for his gentle daughter's sake;
        And never dare misfortune cross her foot,   35
        Unless she do it under this excuse
        That she is issue to a faithless Jew.
        Come, go with me; peruse this as thou goest.
        Fair Jessica shall be my torchbearer.

Exeunt

ACT 2   SCENE 5
Venice   Shylock's house

Enter SHYLOCK and LANCELOT

SHYLOCK Well, thou shalt see, thy eyes shall be thy judge,
        The difference of old Shylock and Bassanio –
        What, Jessica! – Thou shalt not gourmandise
        As thou hast done with me – What, Jessica! –
        And sleep, and snore, and rend apparel out.   5
        Why, Jessica, I say!
LANCELOT   Why, Jessica!
SHYLOCK Who bids thee call? I do not bid thee call.
LANCELOT Your worship was wont to tell me I could do nothing
    without bidding.

Shylock intends to dine with Bassanio, even though he is uneasy because of ominous dreams. He leaves Jessica to protect the house, warning her not to watch the masque. Lancelot tells her of Lorenzo's impending visit.

1 Shylock: why is he agitated? (in groups of three or four)

- One person reads Shylock's two speeches (lines 11–18 and lines 27–38); the others echo any words which reflect Shylock's nervous excitement. Talk about which words seem particularly important in creating his agitated mood.
- Shylock angrily describes how he expects the Christians to behave during the masque (lines 27–38). Make up one example of such behaviour and present it to the rest of the class as a tableau, then talk together about why Shylock might be against such behaviour.
- Is Shylock a spoilsport? Do you think Shakespeare is deliberately or unfairly trying to make the audience dislike Shylock?

2 Inside Shylock's house

Shylock is very conscious of the need to keep his house locked and secure whilst he is away. Imagine that you are designing the set. How would you present Shylock's house on-stage?

3 Shylock's dream (in groups of three or four)

Make up a short mime to show Shylock's dream (line 18). Some directors cut line 18 because they feel it presents Shylock as a stereotype. Would you keep it in or cut it?

4 Nonsense?

Many attempts have been made to explain lines 22–6, but it's probably best to see them as Lancelot talking nonsense to make the audience laugh. What do you think?

---

bid forth invited
prodigal wasteful
loath unwilling
tonight last night
reproach approach (Lancelot's mistake, but Shylock takes him literally)

wry-necked fife a flute (pretend to play a flute and see what happens to your neck)
varnished faces wearing masks
shallow foppery hollow nonsense
Hagar's offspring Ishmael, the outcast son of an Egyptian servant

Enter JESSICA

JESSICA Call you? What is your will?   10
SHYLOCK I am bid forth to supper, Jessica.
       There are my keys. But wherefore should I go?
       I am not bid for love, they flatter me;
       But yet I'll go in hate, to feed upon
       The prodigal Christian. Jessica my girl,   15
       Look to my house. I am right loath to go;
       There is some ill a-brewing towards my rest,
       For I did dream of money bags tonight.
LANCELOT I beseech you, sir, go; my young master doth expect your
    reproach.   20
SHYLOCK So do I his.
LANCELOT And they have conspired together – I will not say you shall
    see a masque; but if you do, then it was not for nothing that my
    nose fell a-bleeding on Black Monday last, at six a clock i'the
    morning, falling out that year on Ash Wednesday was four year in   25
    th'afternoon.
SHYLOCK What, are there masques? Hear you me, Jessica,
       Lock up my doors, and when you hear the drum
       And the vile squealing of the wry-necked fife,
       Clamber not you up to the casements then   30
       Nor thrust your head into the public street
       To gaze on Christian fools with varnished faces;
       But stop my house's ears – I mean my casements –
       Let not the sound of shallow foppery enter
       My sober house. By Jacob's staff I swear   35
       I have no mind of feasting forth tonight:
       But I will go. Go you before me, sirrah;
       Say I will come.
LANCELOT   I will go before, sir.
       [*Aside to Jessica*] Mistress, look out at window for all this:
       There will come a Christian by   40
       Will be worth a Jewès eye   [*Exit*]
SHYLOCK What says that fool of Hagar's offspring, ha?
JESSICA His words were 'Farewell, mistress', nothing else.

Shylock is glad to be rid of Lancelot, whom he sees as a lazy wastrel. Jessica relishes the prospect of escaping from her father. In Scene 6, Gratiano and Salarino await Lorenzo: he is late.

1 A testimonial for Lancelot

In lines 44–9 Shylock talks of his former servant, Lancelot. Imagine that he has been asked to produce an honest reference about Lancelot for his future employer, Bassanio. Write Shylock's reference on Lancelot.

2 Lorenzo and Jessica (in groups of three or four)

Jessica is going to leave her father and elope with Lorenzo. Talk together about who has the most to lose from this elopement: Jessica or Lorenzo? Bear in mind that these young people come from very different backgrounds.

Make up a group tableau which captures the meaning of the final line of Scene 5.

3 Gratiano: a man of pleasure? (in groups of five or six)

Gratiano's lines 9–20 are an elaboration of what Salarino has just said: looking forward to love is more enjoyable than long marriage, so first lovers cannot wait to meet.

Read Gratiano's speech, changing reader at each punctuation mark. Notice how he gives different examples of the same theme. As you read, stress all the words to do with physical sensations and feelings. Talk about the effect you have achieved. Do you agree with what Salarino and Gratiano are saying? Then look back to Nerissa's speech (page 13, lines 3–8) and discuss any ideas the two speeches have in common.

---

patch fool
drones hive not bees that do not work will find no home with me
penthouse overhanging upper storey
make stand wait
O, ten times . . . unforfeited the doves of love favour an engagement more than a long marriage

untread retrace
measures paces
unbated unrestrained
younger a young gentleman
scarfed decked out
strumpet prostitute
ribs ship's timbers
rent torn

SHYLOCK The patch is kind enough, but a huge feeder,
       Snail-slow in profit, and he sleeps by day   45
       More than the wildcat. Drones hive not with me,
       Therefore I part with him, and part with him
       To one that I would have him help to waste
       His borrowed purse. Well, Jessica, go in;
       Perhaps I will return immediately.   50
       Do as I bid you, shut doors after you.
       Fast bind, fast find:
       A proverb never stale in thrifty mind.   *Exit*
JESSICA Farewell, and if my fortune be not crossed,
       I have a father, you a daughter, lost.   *Exit* 55

ACT 2   SCENE 6
Venice   Outside Shylock's house

Enter the masquers, GRATIANO and SALARINO

GRATIANO This is the penthouse under which Lorenzo
       Desired us to make stand.
SALARINO His hour is almost past.
GRATIANO And it is marvel he outdwells his hour,
       For lovers ever run before the clock.   5
SALARINO O, ten times faster Venus' pigeons fly
       To seal love's bonds new made than they are wont
       To keep obligèd faith unforfeited!
GRATIANO That ever holds: who riseth from a feast
       With that keen appetite that he sits down?   10
       Where is the horse that doth untread again
       His tedious measures with the unbated fire
       That he did pace them first? All things that are
       Are with more spirit chasèd than enjoyed.
       How like a younger or a prodigal   15
       The scarfèd bark puts from her native bay,
       Hugged and embracèd by the strumpet wind!
       How like the prodigal doth she return
       With overweathered ribs and ragged sails,
       Lean, rent, and beggared by the strumpet wind!   20

Lorenzo meets his friends outside Shylock's house. Jessica, although embarrassed by her disguise as a boy, is ready to elope with him, having already plundered her father's gold and jewels.

1 'My affairs have made you wait' (in pairs)

Lorenzo's late arrival is in contradiction to all Gratiano has just said about lovers. So why does Shakespeare make Lorenzo late, and what has he been doing whilst the others have been waiting?

2 A tender dialogue (in pairs)

Jessica, still in her father's house, talks to Lorenzo, who is in the street below. Take parts and read lines 27–51, but make sure that you are at some distance from each other. You could also place some kind of barrier or obstacle between you. First, read the lines as tenderly and romantically as possible, then try reading them to stress the physical awkwardness of the situation and the difficulties of communicating. Which version did you prefer?

3 Jessica: a problem of self-image? (in small groups)

Make a list of all Jessica's comments about herself and her appearance in lines 34–51. Talk about what they tell you of her character, and what they suggest of the role of women in Venice.

---

long abode lateness
exchange disguise
light obvious (or wanton)
office of discovery act of
  revelation
garnish disguise or costume
close secretive

stayed for awaited
gild cover in gold
moe more
hood mask or hat
gentle a woman who has been well
  brought up (and also a pun on
  Gentile – a non-Jew)

Enter LORENZO

SALARINO Here comes Lorenzo; more of this hereafter.
LORENZO Sweet friends, your patience for my long abode.
　　　　Not I but my affairs have made you wait.
　　　　When you shall please to play the thieves for wives,
　　　　I'll watch as long for you then. Approach –　　　　　25
　　　　Here dwells my father Jew. Ho! Who's within?

　　　　[Enter] JESSICA *above[, in boy's clothes]*

JESSICA Who are you? Tell me, for more certainty,
　　　　Albeit I'll swear that I do know your tongue.
LORENZO Lorenzo, and thy love.
JESSICA Lorenzo certain, and my love indeed,　　　　　　30
　　　　For who love I so much? And now who knows
　　　　But you, Lorenzo, whether I am yours?
LORENZO Heaven and thy thoughts are witness that thou art.
JESSICA Here, catch this casket, it is worth the pains.
　　　　I am glad 'tis night, you do not look on me,　　　　35
　　　　For I am much ashamed of my exchange.
　　　　But love is blind, and lovers cannot see
　　　　The pretty follies that themselves commit;
　　　　For if they could, Cupid himself would blush
　　　　To see me thus transformèd to a boy.　　　　　　40
LORENZO Descend, for you must be my torchbearer.
JESSICA What, must I hold a candle to my shames?
　　　　They in themselves, good sooth, are too too light.
　　　　Why, 'tis an office of discovery, love,
　　　　And I should be obscured.
LORENZO 　　　　　　　So are you, sweet,　　　　45
　　　　Even in the lovely garnish of a boy.
　　　　But come at once,
　　　　For the close night doth play the runaway,
　　　　And we are stayed for at Bassanio's feast.
JESSICA I will make fast the doors, and gild myself　　　　50
　　　　With some moe ducats, and be with you straight.
　　　　　　　　　　　　　　　　[Exit Jessica above]
GRATIANO Now by my hood, a gentle and no Jew!

Lorenzo talks of his love for Jessica, then elopes with her. Antonio informs Gratiano that Bassanio's ship is about to leave. In Scene 7, the Prince of Morocco considers which casket to choose.

1 What are Gratiano's thoughts? (in pairs)

Gratiano says nothing during the conversation between Jessica and Lorenzo, but he probably has his own views on their relationship. Recall your impression of Gratiano, especially what Bassanio said about his rough manners.

One person slowly reads Lorenzo's lines 53–8. The other, as Gratiano, comments on every line.

2 A letter to Shylock

Imagine that Jessica writes a letter to her father. What's in it?

3 The casket scene

Design the set for Scene 7, the first of the casket scenes. Consider how the process of choosing might be seen as a ceremony or ritual. How can your set help to create that impression?

4 How do they enter? (in groups of ten or twelve)

At the beginning of Scene 7, Portia and Morocco enter with their trains (followers). Talk about how you think the opening three lines should be staged. Should Portia and Morocco enter separately or together? Where do they position themselves to await the unveiling of the caskets? Then try the entrance and unveiling practically in several different ways. Choose which you felt worked best.

5 Which will he choose? (in pairs)

Glance back to the scene where Morocco first appeared (page 33) to remind yourself of your impression of him. Now read lines 4–10, which reveal the inscription on each casket. Before you turn the page, talk together about which one you think he will choose because of his character.

Beshrew me Devil take me (a mild oath)

is come about has changed
several different

LORENZO Beshrew me but I love her heartily.
   For she is wise, if I can judge of her,
   And fair she is, if that mine eyes be true,   55
   And true she is, as she hath proved herself:
   And therefore like herself, wise, fair, and true,
   Shall she be placèd in my constant soul.

     Enter JESSICA

   What, art thou come? On, gentleman, away!
   Our masquing mates by this time for us stay.   60
           Exit [*with Jessica*]

     Enter ANTONIO
ANTONIO Who's there?
GRATIANO Signor Antonio?
ANTONIO Fie, fie, Gratiano, where are all the rest?
   'Tis nine a clock, our friends all stay for you.
   No masque tonight: the wind is come about,   65
   Bassanio presently will go aboard.
   I have sent twenty out to seek for you.
GRATIANO I am glad on't; I desire no more delight
   Than to be under sail and gone tonight.
             Exeunt

ACT 2   SCENE 7
Belmont   A room in Portia's house

Enter PORTIA *with the Prince of* MOROCCO *and both their trains*

PORTIA Go, draw aside the curtains and discover
   The several caskets to this noble prince.
   Now make your choice.
MOROCCO This first of gold, who this inscription bears,
   'Who chooseth me, shall gain what many men desire.'   5
   The second silver, which this promise carries,
   'Who chooseth me, shall get as much as he deserves.'
   This third dull lead, with warning all as blunt,
   'Who chooseth me, must give and hazard all he hath.'
   How shall I know if I do choose the right?   10

Portia reminds Morocco that he can win her hand by choosing the correct casket. Morocco deliberates over the three choices: lead, silver and gold.

1 Morocco ❤ Portia? (in groups of five or six)

First, try a group reading of Morocco's lines 13–60. Each person reads as far as the next punctuation mark, then hands on to the next reader. Continue in this way to the end of the speech. Then choose one or more of the following activities:

- Talk together about how you would stage this soliloquy.
- In lines 39–48, Morocco talks extravagantly about the extremes to which men go to woo Portia. Choose your favourite idea from these lines, and improvise a piece of colourful theatre inspired by it.
- Talk together about whether you think he is 'over-the-top'. Do you think that Morocco exaggerates too much?
- Look at the picture of Portia and Morocco. Which line of Morocco's best fits this moment?

withal as well	**graved** engraved
dross worthless things	**Hyrcanian deserts** open land near
even unbiased	the Caspian Sea
estimation reputation	**throughfares** highways
disabling undervaluing	**watery kingdom** the sea

PORTIA The one of them contains my picture, prince.
If you choose that, then I am yours withal.
MOROCCO Some god direct my judgement! Let me see:
I will survey th'inscriptions back again.
What says this leaden casket?   15
'Who chooseth me, must give and hazard all he hath.'
Must give – for what? For lead? Hazard for lead!
This casket threatens: men that hazard all
Do it in hope of fair advantages.
A golden mind stoops not to shows of dross;   20
I'll then nor give nor hazard aught for lead.
What says the silver with her virgin hue?
'Who chooseth me, shall get as much as he deserves.'
As much as he deserves – pause there, Morocco,
And weigh thy value with an even hand.   25
If thou be'st rated by thy estimation
Thou dost deserve enough; and yet enough
May not extend so far as to the lady;
And yet to be afeared of my deserving
Were but a weak disabling of myself.   30
As much as I deserve: why, that's the lady.
I do in birth deserve her, and in fortunes,
In graces, and in qualities of breeding:
But more than these, in love I do deserve.
What if I strayed no farther, but chose here?   35
Let's see once more this saying graved in gold:
'Who chooseth me, shall gain what many men desire.'
Why, that's the lady; all the world desires her.
From the four corners of the earth they come
To kiss this shrine, this mortal breathing saint.   40
The Hyrcanian deserts and the vasty wilds
Of wide Arabia are as throughfares now
For princes to come view fair Portia.
The watery kingdom, whose ambitious head
Spits in the face of heaven, is no bar   45
To stop the foreign spirits, but they come
As o'er a brook to see fair Portia.
One of these three contains her heavenly picture.

Morocco decides to open the gold casket, hoping to discover Portia's picture inside. However, he finds only a skull and a dismissive message. To Portia's relief, Morocco departs for home.

1 What's inside the casket? (in pairs)

Morocco opens the casket to find a human skull inside. A scroll, with a message on it, is inside one of the eye sockets. Discuss the possible reasons for Shakespeare including these details, then make a drawing of the contents.

2 'All that glisters is not gold' (in pairs)

This is one of the best-known lines in the play, and is often used as a proverb today. Choose any other character in the play who might well be reminded of this saying. Share your ideas, and the reasons for your choice, with another pair.

3 A message to Morocco

Read aloud the words on the scroll (lines 65–73), stressing the rhyme at the end of each line. Now write your own nine-line poem in a similar style. Choose as your theme either Portia's thoughts about Morocco or Morocco's response to the message on the scroll. For the end of each line, be careful to pick words that have lots of possibilities for rhyming.

4 'Let all of his complexion choose me so'
   (in groups of three or four)

Portia's final line could well cause offence to an audience for its racism. If you were directing the play, would you include it or leave it out? Give reasons for your choice, and say how the line adds to your impression of Portia.

---

like likely
rib enclose
cerecloth shroud, a cloth in which
 a corpse was wrapped
immured walled up
tried purified

insculped engraved
thrive prosper
form likeness, picture
carrion death bare skull
inscrolled written down
tedious long-drawn-out

Is't like that lead contains her? 'Twere damnation
To think so base a thought; it were too gross   50
To rib her cerecloth in the òbscure grave.
Or shall I think in silver she's immured,
Being ten times undervalued to tried gold?
O sinful thought! Never so rich a gem
Was set in worse than gold. They have in England   55
A coin that bears the figure of an angel
Stampèd in gold; but that's insculped upon:
But here an angel in a golden bed
Lies all within. Deliver me the key:
Here do I choose, and thrive I as I may.   60

PORTIA There take it, prince, and if my form lie there,
    Then I am yours.
        [Morocco unlocks the gold casket]

MOROCCO   O hell! What have we here?
A carrion death, within whose empty eye
There is a written scroll. I'll read the writing.
    'All that glisters is not gold;   65
    Often have you heard that told.
    Many a man his life hath sold
    But my outside to behold.
    Gilded tombs do worms infold.
    Had you been as wise as bold,   70
    Young in limbs, in judgement old,
    Your answer had not been inscrolled.
    Fare you well, your suit is cold.'
Cold indeed, and labour lost;
Then farewell heat, and welcome frost.   75
Portia, adieu; I have too grieved a heart
To take a tedious leave: thus losers part.
        Exit [Morocco with his train]

PORTIA A gentle riddance! Draw the curtains, go.
Let all of his complexion choose me so.
        Exeunt. [A flourish of cornets]

Bassanio and Gratiano have sailed for Belmont. Jessica, having taken money and jewels, has eloped with Lorenzo. Solanio tells of Shylock's intense anguish at his loss, and suggests that he will seek revenge.

1 'With outcries raised the Duke' (in pairs)

Shylock visits the Duke of Venice to complain about the loss of his daughter and his possessions. He seeks support from the laws of Venice. Shylock manages to persuade the Duke to go with him, intending to search Bassanio's ship.

Improvise Shylock's meeting with the Duke. Concentrate on the reasons why Shylock is aggrieved, his state of mind, and how the Duke receives him.

2 Imagine you are Shylock

Use Solanio's lines 15–22 as the script for Shylock's immediate response to his discovery that Jessica has fled with his money and jewels. You can either act it out or imagine it vividly, section by section, in your mind. Whichever way you choose, speaking the lines aloud will help you to understand and empathise with Shylock's feelings.

3 Sympathy for Shylock? (in groups of five or six)

Solanio and Salarino report, in lines 12–24, what has happened to Shylock. Take it in turns to be Shylock, and use as many of Shylock's own words as possible. The others follow Shylock round the room, mocking and taunting him by ridiculing his words and actions. Everyone take a turn as Shylock.

Afterwards, talk about how you felt as Shylock and what this tells you about his predicament.

Neither Salarino nor Solanio has any sympathy for Shylock. They mock his response to his losses. How do you feel towards them?

---

certified testified to
passion emotional outburst
keep his day fulfil his bond
reasoned chatted

part separate
miscarried was wrecked
fraught laden

Venice

Enter SALARINO and SOLANIO

SALARINO Why, man, I saw Bassanio under sail,
With him is Gratiano gone along;
And in their ship I am sure Lorenzo is not.
SOLANIO The villain Jew with outcries raised the Duke,
Who went with him to search Bassanio's ship.   5
SALARINO He came too late, the ship was under sail.
But there the Duke was given to understand
That in a gondola were seen together
Lorenzo and his amorous Jessica.
Besides, Antonio certified the Duke   10
They were not with Bassanio in his ship.
SOLANIO I never heard a passion so confused,
So strange, outrageous, and so variable,
As the dog Jew did utter in the streets:
'My daughter! O my ducats! O my daughter!   15
Fled with a Christian! O my Christian ducats!
Justice! The law! My ducats and my daughter!
A sealèd bag, two sealèd bags of ducats,
Of double ducats, stolen from me by my daughter!
And jewels – two stones, two rich and precious stones,   20
Stolen by my daughter! Justice! Find the girl!
She hath the stones upon her and the ducats!'
SALARINO Why, all the boys in Venice follow him,
Crying his stones, his daughter, and his ducats.
SOLANIO Let good Antonio look he keep his day,   25
Or he shall pay for this.
SALARINO Marry, well remembered:
I reasoned with a Frenchman yesterday
Who told me, in the Narrow Seas that part
The French and English, there miscarrièd   30
A vessel of our country richly fraught.

Salarino hopes that the shipwrecked galleon was not one of Antonio's. He describes the selfless and loving friendship Antonio has for Bassanio. Scene 9 prepares for the Prince of Arragon's choice of casket.

1 Sixty-second newsflash (in small groups)

You are a reporter for Radio Venice. Compose a brief newsflash on the shipwreck in 'the Narrow Seas' (line 29). You could include interviews with the Frenchman who told Salarino about it, and with Salarino himself. Your report must be no longer than sixty seconds.

2 'I saw Bassanio and Antonio part' (in groups of three)

As one person reads lines 37–50, the other two enact the parting of Bassanio and Antonio, showing all the details described. Can you work out different ways of presenting line 48?

3 Shylock versus Antonio

Scene 8 gives a dramatic impression of the differences between Shylock and Antonio, especially in terms of how they handle the 'loss' of what is dear to them. Make two columns, headed 'Shylock' and 'Antonio', and produce a list of all the contrasting details you can find. Include as much of Shakespeare's language as possible.

When you have completed your lists, review them in the light of the fact that all the information comes from two Christians who are friends of Antonio and detest Shylock. What difference does that make to your interpretation of the differences between Shylock and Antonio? How trustworthy are Salarino and Solanio?

---

slubber perform in a slovenly way
the very . . . time until you have fulfilled your intentions
ostents displays
affection wondrous sensible very strong emotion

quicken enliven
tane taken
election choice
presently at once

I thought upon Antonio when he told me,
And wished in silence that it were not his.
SOLANIO You were best to tell Antonio what you hear.
Yet do not suddenly, for it may grieve him.   35
SALARINO A kinder gentleman treads not the earth.
I saw Bassanio and Antonio part:
Bassanio told him he would make some speed
Of his return: he answered, 'Do not so.
Slubber not business for my sake, Bassanio,   40
But stay the very riping of the time;
And for the Jew's bond which he hath of me,
Let it not enter in your mind of love.
Be merry, and employ your chiefest thoughts
To courtship, and such fair ostents of love   45
As shall conveniently become you there.'
And even there, his eye being big with tears,
Turning his face, he put his hand behind him,
And with affection wondrous sensible
He wrung Bassanio's hand, and so they parted.   50
SOLANIO I think he only loves the world for him.
I pray thee let us go and find him out
And quicken his embracèd heaviness
With some delight or other.
SALARINO   Do we so.

Exeunt

ACT 2   SCENE 9
Belmont   A room in Portia's house

Enter NERISSA and a Servitor

NERISSA Quick, quick, I pray thee, draw the curtain straight.
The Prince of Arragon hath tane his oath,
And comes to his election presently.

The Merchant of Venice

The Prince of Arragon, hoping to win Portia, explains the terms of the oath he has undertaken. He deliberates about his choice of casket.

---

1 'I am enjoined by oath'

Read the Prince of Arragon's lines 9–15. He reports the terms of the oath that all Portia's suitors are made to swear. Produce the actual document, making it as authentic as possible.

2 What is Portia thinking? (in pairs)

Take it in turns to read aloud Arragon's long speech (lines 18–51), pausing at the end of each sentence. As one person reads, the other gives Portia's reaction to each sentence. Questions that will help you are:

- Does Portia already know in which casket her portrait is locked?
- How does she feel about the prospect of being married to Arragon?

3 Newspaper reporter (in small groups)

You are a news reporter with the *Belmont Gazette*. You have been instructed by your editor to cover Arragon's public courtship of Portia (just as modern reporters are asked to cover conferences, summit meetings and Royal weddings). You have a maximum of 200 words and headline space. Summarise the main points made by Arragon in lines 18–51 as he considers which casket to choose. Remain as true as you can to his actual words. Each person prepares a draft. Give this to your partner for comment and sub-editing, then produce the final copy together.

---

nuptial rites marriage ceremony
unfold disclose
injunctions conditions
addressed prepared
ere before
fond foolish

the martlet the swift or house martin
casualty misfortune
jump agree
cozen cheat
stamp of merit genuine merit

[A flourish of cornets.] Enter [the Prince of] ARRAGON, *his train,*
and PORTIA

PORTIA Behold, there stand the caskets, noble prince.
    If you choose that wherein I am contained,   5
    Straight shall our nuptial rites be solemnised;
    But if you fail, without more speech, my lord,
    You must be gone from hence immediately.
ARRAGON I am enjoined by oath to observe three things:
    First, never to unfold to anyone   10
    Which casket 'twas I chose; next, if I fail
    Of the right casket, never in my life
    To woo a maid in way of marriage; lastly,
    If I do fail in fortune of my choice,
    Immediately to leave you and be gone.   15
PORTIA To these injunctions everyone doth swear
    That comes to hazard for my worthless self.
ARRAGON And so have I addressed me. Fortune now
    To my heart's hope! Gold, silver, and base lead.
    'Who chooseth me, must give and hazard all he hath.'   20
    You shall look fairer ere I give or hazard.
    What says the golden chest? Ha, let me see:
    'Who chooseth me, shall gain what many men desire.'
    What many men desire: that 'many' may be meant
    By the fool multitude that choose by show,   25
    Not learning more than the fond eye doth teach,
    Which pries not to th'interior, but like the martlet
    Builds in the weather on the outward wall,
    Even in the force and road of casualty.
    I will not choose what many men desire,   30
    Because I will not jump with common spirits,
    And rank me with the barbarous multitudes.
    Why then, to thee, thou silver treasure house:
    Tell me once more what title thou dost bear.
    'Who chooseth me, shall get as much as he deserves.'   35
    And well said too, for who shall go about
    To cozen Fortune and be honourable
    Without the stamp of merit? Let none presume
    To wear an undeservèd dignity.

Arragon, guided by what he feels he deserves, chooses the silver casket. He finds the portrait of a 'blinking idiot' instead of Portia's picture. Disappointed, he takes his leave.

1 Who's who? (in groups of three or four)

Look at the picture below of Arragon choosing the casket. Work out who the other characters might be.

2 'Too long a pause . . .' (in pairs)

Read line 52 to each other in as many different ways as possible to convey Portia's thoughts and feelings. Decide on which you think is the most appropriate, and share your version with another pair.

---

estates, degrees and offices titles, qualifications and positions
cover wear hats (as a sign of greatness)
that stand bare who take off their hats/go bareheaded

gleaned picked out and rejected
desert what is my right
schedule written scroll
distinct offices separate functions
iwis without doubt
wroth anger and grief

O, that estates, degrees, and offices   40
Were not derived corruptly, and that clear honour
Were purchased by the merit of the wearer!
How many then should cover that stand bare!
How many be commanded that command!
How much low peasantry would then be gleaned   45
From the true seed of honour, and how much honour
Picked from the chaff and ruin of the times
To be new varnished! Well, but to my choice.
'Who chooseth me, shall get as much as he deserves.'
I will assume desert. Give me a key for this,   50
And instantly unlock my fortunes here.
                    [*Arragon unlocks the silver casket*]
PORTIA Too long a pause for that which you find there.
ARRAGON What's here? The portrait of a blinking idiot
          Presenting me a schedule! I will read it.
          How much unlike art thou to Portia!   55
          How much unlike my hopes and my deservings.
          'Who chooseth me, shall have as much as he deserves.'
          Did I deserve no more than a fool's head?
          Is that my prize? Are my deserts no better?
PORTIA To offend and judge are distinct offices,   60
          And of opposèd natures.
ARRAGON   What is here?
                    [*He reads*]
               'The fire seven times tried this;
               Seven times tried that judgement is
               That did never choose amiss.
               Some there be that shadows kiss;   65
               Such have but a shadow's bliss.
               There be fools alive iwis
               Silvered o'er, and so was this.
               Take what wife you will to bed,
               I will ever be your head.   70
               So be gone, you are sped.'
          Still more fool I shall appear
          By the time I linger here.
          With one fool's head I came to woo,
          But I go away with two.   75
          Sweet, adieu; I'll keep my oath,
          Patiently to bear my wroth.   [*Exit Arragon with his train*]

Portia is relieved that Arragon has chosen wrongly. A messenger informs her that a new suitor has arrived from Venice. Nerissa, for Portia's sake, hopes that it is Bassanio.

1 Enter a messenger (in groups of three)

The scene could have ended with Nerissa drawing the curtain across the caskets, but it doesn't. Instead, a messenger tells of the arrival of another lord wishing to seek Portia's hand in marriage. It is also suggested that this lord may be Bassanio. Talk together about why this 'delayed ending' is dramatically effective.

2 More home-spun wisdom from Nerissa
(in groups of five or six)

According to Nerissa, 'Hanging and wiving goes by destiny'. Use this as the title for a short play. You can relate your play to *The Merchant of Venice* or make it a quite separate invention.

3 'Gifts of rich value'

Make a list of appropriate gifts from Bassanio to Portia. Your list should reflect the characters of both Bassanio and Portia, as well as the type of society depicted in the play.

4 A profile of Portia (in pairs)

Portia does not say very much in this scene. Read her speeches aloud to each other – first in a friendly way, then in a sharp, aggressive manner. Then talk together about how this scene helps build up a picture of Portia. What do you think of her behaviour in this scene?

---

deliberate reasoning
They have . . . wit to lose All their wisdom leads only to them choosing wrongly
sensible regreets gifts
to wit thus
commends compliments
breath words

likely promising
costly splendid
forespurrer horseman who goes ahead of the others
kin relation
highday wit fine language
post messenger
so mannerly in such a fetching way

PORTIA Thus hath the candle singed the moth.
    O, these deliberate fools! When they do choose
    They have the wisdom by their wit to lose.   80
NERISSA The ancient saying is no heresy:
    'Hanging and wiving goes by destiny.'
PORTIA Come draw the curtain, Nerissa.

Enter a MESSENGER

MESSENGER Where is my lady?
PORTIA   Here. What would my lord?
MESSENGER Madam, there is alighted at your gate   85
    A young Venetian, one that comes before
    To signify th'approaching of his lord,
    From whom he bringeth sensible regreets:
    To wit, besides commends and courteous breath,
    Gifts of rich value. Yet I have not seen   90
    So likely an ambassador of love.
    A day in April never came so sweet
    To show how costly summer was at hand
    As this forespurrer comes before his lord.
PORTIA No more I pray thee, I am half afeared   95
    Thou wilt say anon he is some kin to thee,
    Thou spend'st such highday wit in praising him.
    Come, come, Nerissa, for I long to see
    Quick Cupid's post that comes so mannerly.
NERISSA Bassanio, Lord Love, if thy will it be!   100
                             Exeunt

Looking back at Act 2
Activities for groups or individuals

1 Fathers and daughters

Conflict between fathers and daughters occurs in many of Shakespeare's plays (Juliet and Capulet in *Romeo and Juliet*; Ophelia and Polonius in *Hamlet*; Cordelia and Lear in *King Lear*; Leonato and Hero in *Much Ado About Nothing*; Cymbeline and Imogen in *Cymbeline*). *The Merchant of Venice* is no exception. In Act 2 both Portia and Jessica try to come to terms with the demands made on them by their fathers.

Explore this father–daughter conflict through a modern medium. Imagine you are producing a daytime TV chat show on 'fathers and daughters'. Interview Portia and Jessica as your special guests. You will need three people to do this – the rest of the class can be the studio audience. Encourage them to ask questions, too!

2 Design the caskets

Shakespeare never tells what the caskets are actually like. He leaves it to the imagination. In one production they were over six feet tall!

Draw or make your own version of the gold, silver and lead caskets. Think carefully about shape, size and design. On pages 68 and 84 are examples of caskets used in two different productions of the play.

3 Re-structuring the play

In many productions, Act 2 Scene 1 and Act 2 Scene 7 are put together and played as one continuous scene. What do you think are the advantages and disadvantages of playing the Morocco scenes in this way?

4 The three suitors . . .

Laurence Olivier had an ingenious idea for the casket scenes. Bassanio should play all three suitors, coming first disguised as Morocco, then as Arragon, and then as himself! What effect would this have on the casket scenes? Do you like the idea?

5 An extra scene

Shylock appears in only five scenes, but some directors give him a sixth which is not in the original script! This is a scene where Shylock returns from supper with the Christians to find that his daughter has deserted him and taken his valuables. In one such production Shylock returns, knocks, enters his house and rushes to all the windows. When he finds the house empty he flings himself on the ground, tears his clothes and sprinkles ashes on his head. Talk together about the value of adding such a scene.

6 Jessica and Shylock

Identify all the scenes which suggest Jessica's relationship with her father.

- What signs are there of love and affection between father and daughter?
- Can you justify one director's decision to have Shylock actually strike Jessica during one of their exchanges?
- How do you see their relationship?

7 Shylock's revenge

The director Jonathan Miller said that Shylock's loss of his daughter is 'the very most appalling disaster that can happen to an orthodox Jewish family'. How important do you think the loss of Jessica is in motivating Shylock's desire for revenge?

8 Changing the scene . . .

In Act 2 there are nine different scenes. Choose one of the following activities:

- Design a set for Act 2 that allows each scene to flow quickly and easily into the next.
- Produce a caption, a headline or a cartoon drawing to catch the essence of each scene.
- Draw a flow diagram that explains how the plot develops in Act 2.

Solanio and Salarino talk of the rumours sweeping the Rialto about Antonio's ship wrecked on the Goodwin Sands. They taunt Shylock about Jessica's elopement. He suspects that they were part of the conspiracy.

1 Shipwrecked on the Goodwins

Salarino gives an eerie description of the Goodwins (a hazardous area in the Straits of Dover). Read lines 3–5, then draw a picture of this dangerous place in the English Channel. Write a caption for the picture based on his words.

2 Radio Venice (in pairs)

Using the details in lines 2–6, produce a radio newsflash about Antonio's latest piece of bad luck. If possible, tape-record your report to broadcast to the rest of the class.

3 Gossip Report (in small groups)

Salarino and Solanio talk about these rumours as if they were told by an old woman called 'gossip Report'. Talk together about what lines 7–9 suggest about the two men's attitudes to women.

4 Enter Shylock (in pairs)

In his 1970 production the director Jonathan Miller had Shylock enter with Jessica's discarded dress in his arms. Talk about the meaning this might have for the audience.

Think up your own ideas for Shylock's entry to give the audience an understanding of how he feels about Jessica's betrayal. How does he move? What are his facial expressions and physical appearance? What other meaningful object could he carry on-stage? Talk through your ideas for making Shylock's entry dramatically powerful. Act out your suggestions.

---

flat sandbanks covered with shallow sea water
knapped ginger munched ginger
slips of prolixity exaggerations of a story
crossing . . . talk going into too much detail

O that . . . company I wish my reputation was as good as his
cross spoil
complexion character
dam mother bird
Rebels . . . years Can't you get an erection?

ACT 3   SCENE I
Venice   A public place

Enter SOLANIO and SALARINO

SOLANIO Now, what news on the Rialto?

SALARINO Why, yet it lives there unchecked that Antonio hath a ship
of rich lading wrecked on the Narrow Seas; the Goodwins I think
they call the place – a very dangerous flat, and fatal, where the
carcases of many a tall ship lie buried, as they say, if my gossip   5
Report be an honest woman of her word.

SOLANIO I would she were as lying a gossip in that as ever knapped
ginger or made her neighbours believe she wept for the death of a
third husband. But it is true, without any slips of prolixity, or
crossing the plain highway of talk, that the good Antonio, the   10
honest Antonio – O that I had a title good enough to keep his name
company! –

SALARINO Come, the full stop.

SOLANIO Ha, what sayest thou? Why, the end is, he hath lost a
ship.   15

SALARINO I would it might prove the end of his losses.

SOLANIO Let me say 'amen' betimes, lest the devil cross my prayer,
for here he comes in the likeness of a Jew.

Enter SHYLOCK

How now, Shylock, what news among the merchants?

SHYLOCK You knew, none so well, none so well as you, of my daugh-   20
ter's flight.

SALARINO That's certain; I for my part knew the tailor that made the
wings she flew withal.

SOLANIO And Shylock for his own part knew the bird was fledged, and
then it is the complexion of them all to leave the dam.   25

SHYLOCK She is damned for it.

SALARINO That's certain – if the devil may be her judge.

SHYLOCK My own flesh and blood to rebel!

SOLANIO Out upon it, old carrion! Rebels it at these years?

SHYLOCK I say my daughter is my flesh and my blood.   30

Shylock speaks menacingly of Antonio and the bond between them. He stresses the common humanity of both Jews and Christians, and says he will learn from Christian example and seek revenge.

1 'I'm the same as you, so I'll do the same as you!'
(in groups of six or seven)

Lines 42–57 are among the most famous in all Shakespeare. To explore Shylock's feelings, choose one or more of the following:

a Stand in a circle and read around the group, changing over at the end of each sentence. Make your first reading angry and revengeful. Then read it again quietly and with dignity, as a plea for understanding and common humanity.

b Two of you are Solanio and Salarino and stand at the opposite end of the room from the rest of the group. The others begin reading the speech in unison, moving towards the two Christians as they speak. Increase the volume the nearer you get to them. Experiment with gesture and tones of voice. Try your best to share and feel Shylock's angry demand for understanding. You'll end up face to face with your opponents, but keep your concentration! Repeat the exercise to give the first Solanio and Salarino a chance to read.

c Repeat activity b, but this time Solanio and Salarino can reply. They should intercut the speech with insults to Shylock taken from this or other parts of the script (see the list on page 169).

d Reduce lines 46–57 to their bare bones. Decide the three most important things Shylock says about himself and his feelings. Compare and talk about your chosen lines with other groups.

e Shakespeare's most famous speeches are usually in verse, yet this one is in prose. Individually or in pairs, re-write different parts of the speech in iambic pentameter (see page 183).

---

jet semi-precious black stone
Rhenish fine white wine
prodigal waster
unto the mart into the market-place
he was wont he liked to

usurer money-lender
forfeit breaks the contract
hindered me stopped me making
what is his humility? How does he take it?
execute commit

SALARINO There is more difference between thy flesh and hers than
between jet and ivory; more between your bloods than there is
between red wine and Rhenish. But tell us, do you hear whether
Antonio have had any loss at sea or no?

SHYLOCK There I have another bad match: a bankrupt, a prodigal, 35
who dare scarce show his head on the Rialto, a beggar that was used
to come so smug upon the mart. Let him look to his bond. He was
wont to call me usurer; let him look to his bond. He was wont to
lend money for a Christian courtesy; let him look to his bond.

SALARINO Why, I am sure if he forfeit thou wilt not take his flesh. 40
What's that good for?

SHYLOCK To bait fish withal; if it will feed nothing else, it will feed my
revenge. He hath disgraced me, and hindered me half a million,
laughed at my losses, mocked at my gains, scorned my nation,
thwarted my bargains, cooled my friends, heated mine enemies – 45
and what's his reason? I am a Jew. Hath not a Jew eyes? Hath not
a Jew hands, organs, dimensions, senses, affections, passions? Fed
with the same food, hurt with the same weapons, subject to the
same diseases, healed by the same means, warmed and cooled by
the same winter and summer as a Christian is? If you prick us, do 50
we not bleed? If you tickle us, do we not laugh? If you poison us,
do we not die? And if you wrong us, shall we not revenge? If we
are like you in the rest, we will resemble you in that. If a Jew wrong
a Christian, what is his humility? Revenge. If a Christian wrong a
Jew, what should his sufferance be by Christian example? Why, 55
revenge! The villainy you teach me I will execute, and it shall go
hard but I will better the instruction.

Enter a [SERVING]MAN *from Antonio*

SERVINGMAN Gentlemen, my master Antonio is at his house, and
desires to speak with you both.

SALARINO We have been up and down to seek him. 60

Enter TUBAL

SOLANIO Here comes another of the tribe; a third cannot be matched,
unless the devil himself turn Jew.

Exeunt [*Salarino and Solanio with the Servingman*]

SHYLOCK How now, Tubal, what news from Genoa? Hast thou found
my daughter?

Shylock rages about the money and jewels Jessica has taken. He wishes her dead. Tubal reports the loss of another of Antonio's ships. Shylock tells him to hire an officer to arrest Antonio.

1 His daughter or his money? (in pairs)

In lines 66–76 Shylock laments his betrayal. But is it the loss of his daughter or his wealth which affects him more? Share a reading of the speech, varying your pace and tone to bring out his real feelings.

2 Tubal: speak the sub-text (in pairs)

Tubal is important because he can give the audience an idea of how Shylock is regarded in the Jewish community. Is he sympathetic, or does he enjoy Shylock's discomfort? Choose parts and read lines 77–98. At the end of each speech, the partner playing Tubal should also speak aloud the thoughts the character might have about giving his news and Shylock's differing reactions to it.

3 Shylock: the Hitler connection (in small groups)

The director Jonathan Miller asked the actor playing Shylock if he recalled seeing a news film of Hitler at the surrender of France. 'Suddenly the Führer was seen dancing a funny little jig of triumph, and I suggested that Olivier [the actor] follow it at the moment when Tubal tells Shylock that Antonio's ships have gone down.' Bearing in mind the abhorrent way Hitler treated the Jews, talk about why you think Miller, who is himself a Jew, gave this direction for lines 80–1.

4 Leah: Mrs Shylock? (in groups of five or six)

Judging by what Shylock says in lines 95–6, Leah seems to have been of great importance to him. Perhaps she was his wife, and therefore Jessica's mother. What do you think?

---

hearsed coffined
lights lands
four score eighty
at a sitting at one go
divers many
break go bankrupt

turquoise turquoise ring
wilderness unlimited number
undone in big trouble
bespeak employ
make what merchandise drive
　what bargain

TUBAL I often came where I did hear of her, but cannot find her.   65

SHYLOCK Why there, there, there, there! A diamond gone cost me two thousand ducats in Frankfurt! The curse never fell upon our nation till now, I never felt it till now. Two thousand ducats in that, and other precious, precious jewels! I would my daughter were dead at my foot, and the jewels in her ear: would she were   70
hearsed at my foot, and the ducats in her coffin. No news of them, why so? And I know not what's spent in the search. Why thou loss upon loss – the thief gone with so much, and so much to find the thief, and no satisfaction, no revenge, nor no ill luck stirring but what lights o'my shoulders, no sighs but o'my breathing, no tears   75
but o'my shedding!

TUBAL Yes, other men have ill luck too. Antonio as I heard in Genoa –

SHYLOCK What, what, what? Ill luck, ill luck?

TUBAL – hath an argosy cast away coming from Tripolis.   80

SHYLOCK I thank God, I thank God. Is it true, is it true?

TUBAL I spoke with some of the sailors that escaped the wreck.

SHYLOCK I thank thee, good Tubal: good news, good news! Ha, ha, heard in Genoa!

TUBAL Your daughter spent in Genoa, as I heard, one night four score   85
ducats.

SHYLOCK Thou stick'st a dagger in me; I shall never see my gold again. Four score ducats at a sitting! Four score ducats!

TUBAL There came divers of Antonio's creditors in my company to Venice that swear he cannot choose but break.   90

SHYLOCK I am very glad of it. I'll plague him, I'll torture him. I am glad of it.

TUBAL One of them showed me a ring that he had of your daughter for a monkey.

SHYLOCK Out upon her! Thou torturest me, Tubal: it was my tur-   95
quoise, I had it of Leah when I was a bachelor. I would not have given it for a wilderness of monkeys.

TUBAL But Antonio is certainly undone.

SHYLOCK Nay, that's true, that very true. Go, Tubal, fee me an officer, bespeak him a fortnight before. I will have the heart of him if he   100
forfeit, for were he out of Venice I can make what merchandise I will. Go, Tubal, and meet me at our synagogue, go, good Tubal, at our synagogue, Tubal.

Exeunt

Portia urges Bassanio to delay before choosing. She could tell him how to choose correctly, but she must not break her oath of secrecy.

---

1 Portia: the first sign of nerves? (in pairs)

Until this scene, Portia has appeared as a composed and confident young woman, but what she says to Bassanio in lines 1–24 lacks her usual assurance and self-control. Read the lines aloud, taking turns to share them between you in any way you feel appropriate. Afterwards, talk together about how an actor in this speech might bring out Portia's feelings for Bassanio. Is Portia's hesitant and ambiguous style how someone in love speaks?

2 Girls should keep quiet! (in groups of four or five)

In line 8 Portia seems to be saying that a woman should keep her feelings of love to herself, perhaps leaving the man to take the initiative. Talk about what this remark adds to your understanding of how women are expected to behave in Venice/Belmont. Are opinions like this still expressed today?

---

trains attendants
tarry wait
forbear be patient
but it . . . love I'm not saying I love you
Hate . . . quality hate doesn't make you feel like that
And yet . . . thought girls must keep their feelings to themselves

I am forsworn I've broken a promise
beshrew curse (playfully)
naughty bad (naughty had a much stronger meaning in Shakespeare's time)
peize slow down
eche add to
election choosing

ACT 3 SCENE 2

Belmont The great hall of Portia's house

Enter BASSANIO, PORTIA, GRATIANO, NERISSA, *and all their trains*

PORTIA I pray you tarry, pause a day or two
Before you hazard, for in choosing wrong
I lose your company; therefore forbear a while.
There's something tells me, but it is not love,
I would not lose you; and you know yourself   5
Hate counsels not in such a quality.
But lest you should not understand me well –
And yet a maiden hath no tongue but thought –
I would detain you here some month or two
Before you venture for me. I could teach you   10
How to choose right, but then I am forsworn.
So will I never be. So may you miss me;
But if you do, you'll make me wish a sin,
That I had been forsworn. Beshrew your eyes!
They have o'erlooked me and divided me: 15
One half of me is yours, the other half yours –
Mine own, I would say: but if mine then yours,
And so all yours. O these naughty times
Puts bars between the owners and their rights!
And so though yours, not yours. Prove it so,   20
Let Fortune go to hell for it, not I.
I speak too long, but 'tis to peize the time,
To eche it, and to draw it out in length,
To stay you from election.

Bassanio is impatient to choose. He and Portia talk playfully of the treachery of love. He insists on choosing without delay. Portia, calling for music, compares him to a dying swan, and to Hercules.

1 Bassanio can't wait!

In lines 24–5 Bassanio is growing impatient and wants to get on with choosing. Think about what was going through his mind while he was listening to Portia, and write down his flow of thought.

2 The treachery of love? (in pairs)

An image of the rack runs through lines 24–38. The rack was an instrument of torture that stretched its victims' limbs. It was often used on traitors to make them confess to treason. Does Portia's interest in the word mean that she is suspicious of Bassanio's love? Read the lines together and decide what you think.

3 Music and language

Portia calls for music to accompany Bassanio's choice, just as music accompanies other important occasions such as coronations or weddings. Music creates atmosphere; so too do words. Select words and phrases from lines 40–62 which set the mood for Bassanio's big decision.

4 Is Portia a victim? (in pairs)

Portia recalls the story of how Hercules (Alcides) rescued the city of Troy from a sea monster which demanded that young girls be sacrificed to it (lines 54–62). She compares herself with these unfortunate young women, as if she were some sort of helpless victim. Talk together about whether or not you agree with Portia's view of herself. Is she serious or is she joking? Or is something else going on?

---

amity friendship
enforced tortured
deliverance being released
aloof away
my eye . . . stream I'll cry a river
flourish fanfare
dulcet sweet

Alcides Hercules
Dardanian wives women of Troy
bleared visages tear-stained faces
the issue of th'exploit the
  outcome of Hercules' fight
fray battle or fight

BASSANIO   Let me choose,
    For as I am, I live upon the rack.   25
PORTIA Upon the rack, Bassanio? Then confess
    What treason there is mingled with your love.
BASSANIO None but that ugly treason of mistrust
    Which makes me fear th'enjoying of my love.
    There may as well be amity and life   30
    'Tween snow and fire, as treason and my love.
PORTIA Ay, but I fear you speak upon the rack
    Where men enforcèd do speak anything.
BASSANIO Promise me life and I'll confess the truth.
PORTIA Well then, confess and live.
BASSANIO   'Confess and love'   35
    Had been the very sum of my confession.
    O happy torment, when my torturer
    Doth teach me answers for deliverance!
    But let me to my fortune and the caskets.
PORTIA Away then! I am locked in one of them: 40
    If you do love me, you will find me out.
    Nerissa and the rest, stand all aloof.
    Let music sound while he doth make his choice;
    Then if he lose he makes a swan-like end,
    Fading in music. That the comparison   45
    May stand more proper, my eye shall be the stream
    And watery deathbed for him. He may win,
    And what is music then? Then music is
    Even as the flourish when true subjects bow
    To a new-crownèd monarch. Such it is   50
    As are those dulcet sounds in break of day,
    That creep into the dreaming bridegroom's ear
    And summon him to marriage. Now he goes
    With no less presence, but with much more love,
    Than young Alcides when he did redeem   55
    The virgin tribute paid by howling Troy
    To the sea-monster. I stand for sacrifice.
    The rest aloof are the Dardanian wives,
    With blearèd visages come forth to view
    The issue of th'exploit. Go, Hercules!   60
    Live thou, I live. With much much more dismay
    I view the fight than thou that mak'st the fray.

As music plays, Bassanio begins making his choice from the caskets.
He considers false appearances in law, religion, war and beauty. In each
case, vice can be concealed beneath a mask of virtue.

1 Make music! (in small groups)

Set the song to music suitable for Bassanio's choosing between the
caskets. Try all kinds of styles: pop, folk, rock, opera, soul – the
choice is yours! Find the version you most enjoy, and share it with the
rest of the class.

By the way, do you think the singer gives a rhyming hint to
Bassanio about which casket to choose in 'bred', 'head', nourish*èd?*

2 Appearances are deceptive (in pairs)

The main theme of lines 73–96 is that people are often different from
how they appear. Bassanio gives examples from a wide range of
human experience. Choose one of his images of deception and
represent it as a tableau to the rest of the class. Hold your image for
about twenty seconds before they begin to guess your choice.

fancy superficial love
begot created
ornament something which
  improves appearance
sober brow serious face
text quotation from a holy book

stayers stairs or ropes
valour's excrement a brave man's
  beard
redoubted feared
crisped curly
wanton playful

[*Here music.*] *A song the whilst Bassanio comments on the caskets to himself*

    Tell me where is fancy bred,
    Or in the heart, or in the head?
    How begot, how nourishèd?   65
     Reply, reply.
    It is engend'red in the eye,
    With gazing fed, and fancy dies
    In the cradle where it lies.
    Let us all ring fancy's knell.   70
    I'll begin it – Ding, dong, bell.
ALL   Ding, dong, bell.
BASSANIO So may the outward shows be least themselves:
    The world is still deceived with ornament.
    In law, what plea so tainted and corrupt   75
    But, being seasoned with a gracious voice,
    Obscures the show of evil? In religion,
    What damnèd error but some sober brow
    Will bless it and approve it with a text,
    Hiding the grossness with fair ornament?   80
    There is no vice so simple but assumes
    Some mark of virtue on his outward parts.
    How many cowards whose hearts are all as false
    As stayers of sand, wear yet upon their chins
    The beards of Hercules and frowning Mars, 85
    Who inward searched have livers white as milk,
    And these assume but valour's excrement
    To render them redoubted. Look on beauty,
    And you shall see 'tis purchased by the weight,
    Which therein works a miracle in nature,   90
    Making them lightest that wear most of it.
    So are those crispèd snaky golden locks
    Which maketh such wanton gambols with the wind
    Upon supposèd fairness, often known
    To be the dowry of a second head,   95
    The skull that bred them in the sepulchre.

Bassanio rejects the gold and silver caskets because he fears that their fine appearance might be misleading. To Portia's delight, he chooses the lead casket. Inside he finds her portrait and a scroll.

1 Bassanio and the lead casket (in small groups)

Some people argue that Bassanio behaves out of character in choosing the lead casket because of his shady past and his motives for marrying Portia (see pages 9–13). Someone like that would more probably go for gold or silver! Talk about whether or not his choice is believable. Does it show that he is a genuine and sincere lover, not a fortune-hunter?

2 Silver and gold (in pairs)

In lines 101–4 Bassanio has harsh words for gold and silver. In Greek mythology, everything King Midas touched, even his food, turned to gold. Silver is the servant of trade between men (but why not women?). Choose either gold or silver and represent Bassanio's words in a tableau, mime or drawing.

3 Bassanio goes over the top (in pairs)

Lines 114–29 show Bassanio to be overjoyed to find Portia's portrait. He certainly uses exaggerated, high-flown language (hyperbole or 'hype') to describe her. Try a live reading of the speech, but use your partner as the subject. This has hilarious possibilities!

You could try your hand at inventing hyperbole (overstatements). What about 'hyperbolising' your thoughts on school dinner, the dress sense of the teaching staff, or a particularly tacky type of motor car? The choice is yours.

---

guilèd treacherous
eloquence fine appearance
fleet to air disappear into thin air
allay reduce
scant ration
surfeit have too much

sunder keep apart
unfurnished without a companion
substance meaning
underprizing not describing adequately
continent the contents

Thus ornament is but the guilèd shore
To a most dangerous sea; the beauteous scarf
Veiling an Indian beauty; in a word,
The seeming truth which cunning times put on   100
To entrap the wisest. Therefore thou gaudy gold,
Hard food for Midas, I will none of thee,
Nor none of thee, thou pale and common drudge
'Tween man and man. But thou, thou meagre lead
Which rather threaten'st than dost promise aught,   105
Thy paleness moves me more than eloquence:
And here choose I. Joy be the consequence!

PORTIA [*Aside*] How all the other passions fleet to air:
As doubtful thoughts, and rash-embraced despair,
And shudd'ring fear, and green-eyed jealousy!   110
O love, be moderate, allay thy ecstasy,
In measure rain thy joy, scant this excess!
I feel too much thy blessing: make it less
For fear I surfeit.
                    [*Bassanio opens the leaden casket*]

BASSANIO   What find I here?
Fair Portia's counterfeit! What demi-god   115
Hath come so near creation? Move these eyes?
Or whether riding on the balls of mine
Seem they in motion? Here are severed lips
Parted with sugar breath; so sweet a bar
Should sunder such sweet friends. Here in her hairs   120
The painter plays the spider, and hath woven
A golden mesh t'entrap the hearts of men
Faster than gnats in cobwebs. But her eyes –
How could he see to do them? Having made one,
Methinks it should have power to steal both his   125
And leave itself unfurnished. Yet look how far
The substance of my praise doth wrong this shadow
In underprizing it, so far this shadow
Doth limp behind the substance. Here's the scroll,
The continent and summary of my fortune.   130

The scroll confirms that Bassanio has won Portia. He asks her to approve the casket's truth. She wishes for his sake that she was a better and wealthier woman.

---

1 The scroll

Shakespeare gives us the words that Bassanio reads, but what does the scroll actually look like? Produce your own version. Make it as authentic as possible.

2 Bassanio's verse (in pairs)

Bassanio speaks three types of verse:

blank verse for lines 114–30
the simple four-beat rhyme of the scroll
rhyming couplets for 139–48.

Talk about possible reasons for using a variety of verse forms. The variation of styles hasn't happened by accident! (You will find help on page 183.)

3 'Her lord, her governor, her king' (in small groups)

Share a group reading of lines 149–74, in which Portia gives a very modest impression of herself. Is she wise to talk about herself in this way at the start of her life-long relationship with Bassanio? On a large sheet of paper, draw up a list of 'do's' and 'don'ts' for Portia at this vital time in her life.

---

by note as instructed
peals loud sounds
ratified approved

livings possessions, wealth
in gross in full

[*He reads*]
'You that choose not by the view
Chance as fair, and choose as true.
Since this fortune falls to you,
Be content and seek no new.
If you be well pleased with this,   135
And hold your fortune for your bliss,
Turn you where your lady is,
And claim her with a loving kiss.'
A gentle scroll! Fair lady, by your leave,
I come by note to give, and to receive.   140
Like one of two contending in a prize
That thinks he hath done well in people's eyes,
Hearing applause and universal shout,
Giddy in spirit, still gazing in a doubt
Whether those peals of praise be his or no –   145
So, thrice-fair lady, stand I even so,
As doubtful whether what I see be true,
Until confirmed, signed, ratified by you.
PORTIA You see me, Lord Bassanio, where I stand,
Such as I am. Though for myself alone   150
I would not be ambitious in my wish
To wish myself much better, yet for you
I would be trebled twenty times myself,
A thousand times more fair, ten thousand times
More rich, that only to stand high in your account   155
I might in virtues, beauties, livings, friends,
Exceed account. But the full sum of me
Is sum of something: which to term in gross
Is an unlessoned girl, unschooled, unpractised;
Happy in this, she is not yet so old   160
But she may learn; happier than this,
She is not bred so dull but she can learn;
Happiest of all, is that her gentle spirit
Commits itself to yours to be directed
As from her lord, her governor, her king.   165

Portia gives herself and all her wealth to Bassanio. She hands him a ring, saying its loss will mark the end of his love. Bassanio swears to wear it until his dying day. Gratiano asks for permission to marry Nerissa.

1 Speak with Portia (whole class)

Portia quite literally gives herself to Bassanio (lines 166–7). What is your reaction to her attitude to her future husband? Each person makes a list of questions to ask Portia about her relationship with Bassanio. One volunteer takes the role of Portia to be questioned ('hot-seated') by the class. If Portia finds a question too difficult, she should say 'Time out', and possible answers can be discussed by everyone.

2 'With this ring . . .'

As was Elizabethan custom, Portia gives Bassanio a ring as a sign of her submission to him. Design an appropriate symbol or engraving for the ring. You could choose some of Portia's words from lines 166–74 as an inscription.

3 Another pair of lovers (in pairs)

Talk together about why you think Shakespeare chose to follow Bassanio and Portia's betrothal with that of Gratiano and Nerissa (lines 186–202). What effect does this have on the mood of the scene at this point?

4 Gratiano and Nerissa: what were they thinking?

Gratiano and Nerissa's wedding plans depended on the outcome of Bassanio's choosing between the caskets. As Gratiano or Nerissa, write your account of the scene up to this point. You've had to listen to a great deal of talking while waiting for Bassanio's decision!

---

presage give warning of, foretell
vantage . . . you opportunity to
  show you up
bereft deprived
oration speech
wild of nothing loud hubbub

our . . . prosper our dreams come
  true
solemnise . . . faith get married
for intermission . . . than you I
  found a wife as quickly as you
as . . . falls by chance

Myself, and what is mine, to you and yours
Is now converted. But now I was the lord
Of this fair mansion, master of my servants,
Queen o'er myself; and even now, but now,
This house, these servants, and this same myself   170
Are yours, my lord's. I give them with this ring,
Which when you part from, lose, or give away,
Let it presage the ruin of your love,
And be my vantage to exclaim on you.
BASSANIO Madam, you have bereft me of all words.   175
Only my blood speaks to you in my veins,
And there is such confusion in my powers
As after some oration fairly spoke
By a belovèd prince there doth appear
Among the buzzing, pleasèd multitude,   180
Where every something being blent together
Turns to a wild of nothing, save of joy
Expressed, and not expressed. But when this ring
Parts from this finger, then parts life from hence:
O then be bold to say Bassanio's dead!   185
NERISSA My lord and lady, it is now our time,
That have stood by and seen our wishes prosper,
To cry 'good joy'. Good joy, my lord and lady!
GRATIANO My lord Bassanio, and my gentle lady,
I wish you all the joy that you can wish;   190
For I am sure you can wish none from me.
And when your honours mean to solemnise
The bargain of your faith, I do beseech you
Even at that time I may be married too.
BASSANIO With all my heart, so thou canst get a wife.   195
GRATIANO I thank your lordship, you have got me one.
My eyes, my lord, can look as swift as yours:
You saw the mistress, I beheld the maid.
You loved, I loved; for intermission
No more pertains to me, my lord, than you.   200
Your fortune stood upon the caskets there,
And so did mine too as the matter falls.

Gratiano gives an account of wooing Nerissa. Lorenzo, Jessica and Salerio arrive, having met on the way to Belmont.

---

1 What did Nerissa say? (in pairs)

It seems that Gratiano had a hard time courting Nerissa (lines 203–8). However, it is only he who gives details of the engagement; Nerissa is hardly given the chance to speak! What would she say about the affair?

Improvise a later conversation between Nerissa and Portia in which Nerissa explains how she was won over by Gratiano.

2 Gratiano wants a son (in pairs)

Gratiano may be joking about his proposed bet with Bassanio and Portia (line 214), but it shows that he values sons more than daughters. Talk together about reasons he might have for this attitude.

3 Jessica un-named (in small groups)

Line 217 is the only 'welcome' to Jessica on her arrival, yet Lorenzo and Salerio are both greeted by name. Talk together about possible reasons for Portia and Bassanio apparently ignoring Jessica.

---

my very roof the roof of my mouth
We'll play . . . ducats we'll bet
  them a thousand ducats that we
  have the first son
stake down lay a bet
infidel non-Christian

If . . . welcome If I'm not too new
  in my job here to greet you
entreat beg
commends . . . you sends you his
  regards
estate situation

For wooing here until I sweat again,
And swearing till my very roof was dry
With oaths of love, at last – if promise last –   205
I got a promise of this fair one here
To have her love, provided that your fortune
Achieved her mistress.
PORTIA   Is this true, Nerissa?
NERISSA Madam, it is, so you stand pleased withal.
BASSANIO And do you, Gratiano, mean good faith?   210
GRATIANO Yes 'faith, my lord.
BASSANIO Our feast shall be much honoured in your marriage.
GRATIANO We'll play with them the first boy for a thousand
    ducats.
NERISSA What, and stake down?   215
GRATIANO No, we shall ne'er win at that sport and stake down.
        But who comes here? Lorenzo and his infidel!
        What, and my old Venetian friend Salerio!

Enter LORENZO, JESSICA, *and* SALERIO, *a messenger from Venice*

BASSANIO Lorenzo and Salerio, welcome hither –
        If that the youth of my new interest here   220
        Have power to bid you welcome. By your leave
        I bid my very friends and countrymen,
        Sweet Portia, welcome.
PORTIA   So do I, my lord.
        They are entirely welcome.
LORENZO I thank your honour. For my part, my lord,   225
        My purpose was not to have seen you here,
        But meeting with Salerio by the way
        He did entreat me past all saying nay
        To come with him along.
SALERIO   I did, my lord,
        And I have reason for it. [*Giving letter*] Signor Antonio   230
        Commends him to you.
BASSANIO   Ere I ope his letter,
        I pray you tell me how my good friend doth.
SALERIO Not sick, my lord, unless it be in mind,
        Nor well, unless in mind: his letter there
        Will show you his estate.   235

93

Bassanio reads Antonio's letter, turning pale as he learns the bad news. He tells Portia of the debt he owes to Antonio, and asks Salerio to confirm the news of Antonio's shipwrecked vessels.

1 Antonio's letter: a prediction (in pairs)

Bassanio reads the letter from Antonio, but does not reveal exactly what it says until later in the scene. Use any clues you can find on the page opposite to work out what the letter might say. Share your ideas, then read the actual letter on page 99. Were you right?

2 'Nerissa, cheer yond stranger, bid her welcome . . . ' (in pairs)

Nerissa is instructed by Gratiano to welcome Jessica. Improvise the conversation between Nerissa and Jessica. Share it with the rest of the class.

In one production of the play, Nerissa was horrified by Gratiano's order. Talk together about the possible reasons for such a reaction from Nerissa.

3 'What, worse and worse?' (in groups of three or four)

There is a change of mood as Bassanio reads Antonio's bad news. The atmosphere of joy and triumph gives way to one of tension and concern.

First, read all the lines on the page opposite. Then, as a director, work out how you would show this change of mood to the audience.

Remember that you can rely on more than the language of the play. Think about the use of lighting and music. How might Gratiano, Salerio, Portia and Bassanio respond as the bad tidings from Venice sink in?

Jason see pages 10–11
shrewd unpleasant
rating valuing
braggart boaster

mere deadly
hit success
'scape escape

[Bassanio] opens the letter

GRATIANO Nerissa, cheer yond stranger, bid her welcome.
    Your hand, Salerio; what's the news from Venice?
    How doth that royal merchant, good Antonio?
    I know he will be glad of our success;
    We are the Jasons, we have won the fleece.   240
SALERIO I would you had won the fleece that he hath lost.
PORTIA There are some shrewd contents in yond same paper
    That steals the colour from Bassanio's cheek:
    Some dear friend dead, else nothing in the world
    Could turn so much the constitution   245
    Of any constant man. What, worse and worse?
    With leave, Bassanio, I am half yourself
    And I must freely have the half of anything
    That this same paper brings you.
BASSANIO   O sweet Portia,
    Here are a few of the unpleasant'st words   250
    That ever blotted paper. Gentle lady,
    When I did first impart my love to you,
    I freely told you all the wealth I had
    Ran in my veins: I was a gentleman.
    And then I told you true; and yet, dear lady,   255
    Rating myself at nothing, you shall see
    How much I was a braggart. When I told you
    My state was nothing, I should then have told you
    That I was worse than nothing; for indeed
    I have engaged myself to a dear friend,   260
    Engaged my friend to his mere enemy,
    To feed my means. Here is a letter, lady,
    The paper as the body of my friend,
    And every word in it a gaping wound
    Issuing lifeblood. But is it true, Salerio?   265
    Hath all his ventures failed? What, not one hit?
    From Tripolis, from Mexico, and England,
    From Lisbon, Barbary, and India,
    And not one vessel 'scape the dreadful touch
    Of merchant-marring rocks?

Salerio confirms that all Antonio's ships are wrecked. He and Jessica tell of Shylock's burning desire to pursue the case against Antonio. Portia offers to cancel Antonio's debt and pay generous interest to Shylock.

1 Shylock meets the Duke of Venice (in pairs)

Salerio reports how Shylock plagues the Duke of Venice incessantly in an attempt to have his case against Antonio dealt with fairly. Improvise one of the meetings between the two characters. Think carefully about Shylock's current mood and his relationship with the ruler of Venice – whom we haven't yet met!

2 'Twenty merchants, / The Duke himself, and the magnificoes' (whole class)

Salerio tells us that all these people tried to persuade Shylock to release Antonio from his bond. As a whole class, reconstruct this scene. First, in small groups, discuss the questions and points these important people would raise with Shylock. Then, as a whole class, 'hot-seat' Shylock. Invent names for your character as merchant or magnifico. Your task is to persuade Shylock to let Antonio off the hook.

3 Jessica

Jessica speaks only once in this scene (lines 283–9). She talks about her father and Antonio. Her elopement and marriage are never mentioned, Portia does not speak to her, and she listens in silence to Salerio's scornful words about her father. Write her diary entry, telling her feelings on arriving at Belmont.

4 Portia: a woman who knows her own mind? (in pairs)

Portia's speech (lines 297–313) consists of eleven sentences. Seven of them are 'orders' and the others are emphatic statements. Read the lines to each other – first in a 'bossy' way, then in a different way. Talk together about what new aspects of her character they reveal.

---

discharge repay
plies plagues
impeach call in question
magnificoes of greatest port most important citizens

courtesies kind deeds
deface cancel

SALERIO   Not one, my lord.   270
          Besides, it should appear that if he had
          The present money to discharge the Jew,
          He would not take it. Never did I know
          A creature that did bear the shape of man
          So keen and greedy to confound a man.   275
          He plies the Duke at morning and at night,
          And doth impeach the freedom of the state
          If they deny him justice. Twenty merchants,
          The Duke himself, and the magnificoes
          Of greatest port have all persuaded with him,   280
          But none can drive him from the envious plea
          Of forfeiture, of justice, and his bond.
JESSICA When I was with him, I have heard him swear
          To Tubal and to Chus, his countrymen,
          That he would rather have Antonio's flesh   285
          Than twenty times the value of the sum
          That he did owe him; and I know, my lord,
          If law, authority, and power deny not
          It will go hard with poor Antonio.
PORTIA Is it your dear friend that is thus in trouble?   290
BASSANIO The dearest friend to me, the kindest man,
          The best conditioned and unwearied spirit
          In doing courtesies; and one in whom
          The ancient Roman honour more appears
          Than any that draws breath in Italy.   295
PORTIA What sums owes he the Jew?
BASSANIO For me, three thousand ducats.
PORTIA   What, no more?
          Pay him six thousand, and deface the bond.
          Double six thousand, and then treble that,
          Before a friend of this description   300
          Shall lose a hair through Bassanio's fault.
          First go with me to church, and call me wife,
          And then away to Venice to your friend!
          For never shall you lie by Portia's side
          With an unquiet soul. You shall have gold   305
          To pay the petty debt twenty times over.

97

Portia orders Bassanio to Venice to help Antonio. Bassanio reads Antonio's letter explaining his dreadful predicament. In Scene 3, Shylock orders the jailer to guard Antonio closely.

1 'I will love you dear' (in pairs)

In line 312 Portia puns on the word 'dear'. This catches one of the main tensions of this scene (and the whole play): how far can money and love live comfortably together? Talk to each other about the relationship between Portia and Bassanio, and whether you think they really do love each other or whether Bassanio still sees Portia as a 'lady richly left'.

2 Antonio and Bassanio (in groups of two or three)

Look back at the last three pages of script and make a note of all the references to Antonio's relationship with Bassanio. Recall their relationship in Act 1. Talk about the kind of friendship Antonio and Bassanio share.

3 Bassanio's letter

Imagine that Bassanio sends ahead of him a letter in response to Antonio's. Write Bassanio's letter.

4 How did the conversation start? (in groups of four)

Scene 3 begins with a conversation already in progress. The jailer has probably been talking with Shylock before they enter. Improvise how the conversation started. According to Shylock, in line 1, someone mentioned 'mercy'! Remember there are four characters involved: Shylock, Solanio, Antonio and the jailer. Involve them all in the conversation.

---

miscarried been wrecked
Nor rest . . . us twain I shall not
  sleep until we meet again

gratis free of interest
fond foolish or compassionate

When it is paid, bring your true friend along.
My maid Nerissa and myself meantime
Will live as maids and widows. Come away,
For you shall hence upon your wedding day.   310
Bid your friends welcome, show a merry cheer;
Since you are dear bought, I will love you dear.
But let me hear the letter of your friend.

BASSANIO [*Reads*] 'Sweet Bassanio, my ships have all miscarried, my
creditors grow cruel, my estate is very low; my bond to the Jew is   315
forfeit, and since in paying it, it is impossible I should live, all debts
are cleared between you and I if I might but see you at my death.
Notwithstanding, use your pleasure; if your love do not persuade
you to come, let not my letter.'

PORTIA O love! Dispatch all business and be gone.   320

BASSANIO Since I have your good leave to go away,
I will make haste. But till I come again
No bed shall e'er be guilty of my stay
Nor rest be interposer 'twixt us twain.

Exeunt

ACT 3   SCENE 3
Venice   A street

Enter SHYLOCK, SOLANIO, ANTONIO, and the Jailer

SHYLOCK Jailer, look to him. Tell not me of mercy.
This is the fool that lent out money gratis.
Jailer, look to him.

ANTONIO   Hear me yet, good Shylock –

SHYLOCK I'll have my bond, speak not against my bond;
I have sworn an oath that I will have my bond.   5
Thou call'dst me dog before thou hadst a cause,
But since I am a dog, beware my fangs.
The Duke shall grant me justice. I do wonder,
Thou naughty jailer, that thou art so fond
To come abroad with him at his request.   10

ANTONIO I pray thee hear me speak –

Antonio suspects that Shylock wants him dead because he has paid the debts of many of Shylock's clients. He feels that the Duke must uphold the law of Venice, and so is resigned to death.

1 Shylock: hogging the conversation . . . (in pairs)

Before he leaves, Shylock dominates the dialogue – Antonio struggles to get a word in. Try reading the exchange aloud (lines 1–17). Shylock should circle around Antonio, delivering each short sentence from a different angle to increase its power. Try it again with Shylock jabbing his finger sharply towards Antonio as he speaks. Work out different ways of conveying Shylock's dominant mood.

2 Solanio's thoughts

Solanio does not speak until Shylock has left. What has he been thinking whilst listening to Shylock and Antonio? Write down his stream of thoughts as he observes the two characters.

3 Questioning Antonio (whole class)

Each person makes a list of points to ask Antonio. A volunteer Antonio can be told some questions in advance of the 'hot-seating'.

4 Antonio's thoughts in prison

Antonio is going back to prison to await his trial the following day. He hopes that Bassanio will arrive in time 'to see me pay his debt'. Imagine that you are Antonio, in your prison cell, the night before your trial. Write down your thoughts in what you fear will be the last entry you will ever make in your diary.

---

intercessors people who plead for others
bootless hopeless
forfeitures penalties (for breaking a contract)

commodity trade
impeach discredit
bated weakened

SHYLOCK I'll have my bond; I will not hear thee speak;
      I'll have my bond, and therefore speak no more.
      I'll not be made a soft and dull-eyed fool,
      To shake the head, relent, and sigh, and yield   15
      To Christian intercessors. Follow not!
      I'll have no speaking, I will have my bond.   *Exit*
SOLANIO It is the most impenetrable cur
      That ever kept with men.
ANTONIO   Let him alone.
      I'll follow him no more with bootless prayers.   20
      He seeks my life, his reason well I know:
      I oft delivered from his forfeitures
      Many that have at times made moan to me;
      Therefore he hates me.
SOLANIO   I am sure the Duke
      Will never grant this forfeiture to hold.   25
ANTONIO The Duke cannot deny the course of law;
      For the commodity that strangers have
      With us in Venice, if it be denied,
      Will much impeach the justice of the state,
      Since that the trade and profit of the city   30
      Consisteth of all nations. Therefore go.
      These griefs and losses have so bated me
      That I shall hardly spare a pound of flesh
      Tomorrow to my bloody creditor.
      Well, jailer, on. Pray God Bassanio come   35
      To see me pay his debt, and then I care not.

                              Exeunt

Lorenzo and Portia talk of the close friendship between Antonio and Bassanio. Portia says she plans to stay in a convent during Bassanio's absence. She appoints Lorenzo master of her household until her return.

1 Point out who's who (in groups of four)

Stand in a circle. One student slowly reads Lorenzo's speech (lines 1–9). The others take the roles of Portia, Bassanio and Antonio. All students point at everyone mentioned on *every* mention – e.g. there are three 'points' in line 1. (This pointing is called deixis. It sounds complicated, but is quickly mastered and will help your understanding of other passages in the play.)

2 Is Lorenzo a creep? (in groups of three or four)

Lorenzo's opening lines (1–4) praise Portia fulsomely. Talk together about the possible reasons why he is so excessive in his praise of Portia's qualities. Do you think he is being sincere, or is he overdoing the praise?

3 Friends resemble each other (in pairs)

The language of both characters in lines 1–21 is very formal and polite. Lorenzo says that if Portia knew what Antonio was truly like, she would be even prouder of her action in helping him. Portia replies (lines 11–18) that because close friends are always alike, Antonio must be like Bassanio in appearance, manner and spirit. But do you agree with Portia? Talk together about whether close friends *are* like each other. Or do you choose your friends because they are unlike you?

---

conceit understanding
amity friendship
customary bounty habitual
  generosity or kindness
egal yoke equal sharing

lineaments appearance
bosom lover closest friend
husbandry and manage daily
  running of a household

ACT 3   SCENE 4
Belmont   A room in Portia's house

Enter PORTIA, NERISSA, LORENZO, JESSICA, *and* BALTHAZAR,
a man of Portia's

LORENZO Madam, although I speak it in your presence,
You have a noble and a true conceit
Of god-like amity, which appears most strongly
In bearing thus the absence of your lord.
But if you knew to whom you show this honour,   5
How true a gentleman you send relief,
How dear a lover of my lord your husband,
I know you would be prouder of the work
Than customary bounty can enforce you.
PORTIA I never did repent for doing good,   10
Nor shall not now; for in companions
That do converse and waste the time together,
Whose souls do bear an egal yoke of love,
There must be needs a like proportion
Of lineaments, of manners, and of spirit;   15
Which makes me think that this Antonio,
Being the bosom lover of my lord,
Must needs be like my lord. If it be so,
How little is the cost I have bestowed
In purchasing the semblance of my soul   20
From out the state of hellish cruelty!
This comes too near the praising of myself,
Therefore no more of it: hear other things.
Lorenzo, I commit into your hands
The husbandry and manage of my house   25
Until my lord's return; for mine own part
I have toward heaven breathed a secret vow
To live in prayer and contemplation,
Only attended by Nerissa here,
Until her husband and my lord's return.   30

Portia says she and Nerissa will stay at a convent. She sends her servant,
Balthazar, to Padua to collect clothes and papers from Doctor Bellario.

---

1 Portia and Jessica (in pairs)

Brief though it is, Jessica eventually manages to speak a line to Portia.
Work on lines 42–4, reading the words aloud in different ways. Use
gestures and movements to illustrate their relationship (or lack of
one). In the English Shakespeare Company's 1991 production, Portia
forgot Jessica's name at line 44 and had to be reminded of it. Try that
version in your own explorations and discuss what point it makes
about the relationship between the two women.

2 Jessica, temporary mistress of Belmont (in pairs)

Jessica will stand in for Portia as the mistress of Belmont while Portia
is absent. As a Jew, she is now in charge of a Christian household.
Improvise a scene where she shares her feelings about this responsibility with her husband Lorenzo.

3 Balthazar: the honest steward

Although he has been on-stage from the beginning of this scene,
nothing is known abut Balthazar except that Portia has always found
him 'honest-true'. Tell or write the story of the good deeds that
Balthazar has previously done for Portia to win her trust.

4 The mystery letter: a prediction
(in groups of three or four)

Balthazar is to take a letter from Portia to Doctor Bellario in Padua.
In reply, she expects 'notes and garments'. Make predictions about
what she is planning.

---

monastery convent
imposition duty
traject place for boarding the ferry

There is a monastery two miles off,
And there we will abide. I do desire you
Not to deny this imposition,
The which my love and some necessity
Now lays upon you.
LORENZO   Madam, with all my heart   35
I shall obey you in all fair commands.
PORTIA My people do already know my mind,
And will acknowledge you and Jessica
In place of Lord Bassanio and myself.
So fare you well till we shall meet again.   40
LORENZO Fair thoughts and happy hours attend on you.
JESSICA I wish your ladyship all heart's content.
PORTIA I thank you for your wish, and am well pleased
To wish it back on you: fare you well, Jessica.
                              Exeunt [Jessica and Lorenzo]
Now, Balthazar –   45
As I have ever found thee honest-true,
So let me find thee still; take this same letter,
And use thou all th'endeavour of a man
In speed to Padua. See thou render this
Into my cousin's hand, Doctor Bellario;   50
And look, what notes and garments he doth give thee
Bring them, I pray thee, with imagined speed
Unto the traject, to the common ferry
Which trades to Venice. Waste no time in words
But get thee gone; I shall be there before thee.   55
BALTHAZAR Madam, I go with all convenient speed.   *[Exit]*
PORTIA Come on, Nerissa; I have work in hand
That you yet know not of. We'll see our husbands
Before they think of us.
NERISSA   Shall they see us?

Portia tells Nerissa of her plans. They will see their husbands again, but in disguise as men. In Scene 5, Lancelot fears that Jessica will be damned because she is a Jew's daughter.

1 Portia and Nerissa in disguise (in pairs)

As Portia shares her plans with Nerissa, she gives us a range of images of typical male behaviour in lines 65–76. Work independently at first. Choose one of these images and practise or mime it for your partner to identify. Then work together on a single image that you will present to the rest of the class. Can the others recognise which image you choose?

2 Portia's view of men

Write a short account of Portia's view of men as revealed in lines 65–76. Show how her words add to your understanding of Portia's attitudes.

3 Manly behaviour (in small groups)

'A thousand raw tricks . . . which I will practise.'

Make a list of five other habits or types of behaviour that the two women might adopt if they are going to convince other people of their 'manhood'. Your list may be serious or, like Portia's, mocking and satirical. Share your ideas with others in the class. Afterwards, try to re-write your list in the same style and rhythm as lines 65–76.

4 Is Portia as innocent as she seems? (in pairs)

On two occasions Portia shows that she is fully alert to sexuality. Lines 61–2, 'accomplished/With that we lack', means 'equipped with male genitals'. Then, in response to Nerissa's question (lines 79–80), she deliberately misunderstands the word 'turn', interpreting it as 'sexually invite'. Talk together about what this adds to your understanding of Portia's character.

---

a habit clothes
accoutred dressed
'frays disputes, fights

quaint ingenious
bragging jacks boastful young men
lewd dirty-minded

PORTIA They shall, Nerissa, but in such a habit   60
      That they shall think we are accomplishèd
      With that we lack. I'll hold thee any wager,
      When we are both accoutred like young men
      I'll prove the prettier fellow of the two,
      And wear my dagger with the braver grace,   65
      And speak between the change of man and boy
      With a reed voice, and turn two mincing steps
      Into a manly stride; and speak of 'frays
      Like a fine bragging youth; and tell quaint lies
      How honourable ladies sought my love,   70
      Which I denying, they fell sick and died –
      I could not do withal. Then I'll repent,
      And wish for all that that I had not killed them;
      And twenty of these puny lies I'll tell,
      That men shall swear I have discontinued school   75
      Above a twelvemonth. I have within my mind
      A thousand raw tricks of these bragging jacks,
      Which I will practise.
NERISSA   Why, shall we turn to men?
PORTIA Fie, what a question's that,
      If thou wert near a lewd interpreter!   80
      But come, I'll tell thee all my whole device
      When I am in my coach, which stays for us
      At the park gate; and therefore haste away,
      For we must measure twenty miles today.   *Exeunt*

ACT 3   SCENE 5
Belmont   Portia's garden

Enter LANCELOT the Clown and JESSICA

LANCELOT Yes truly, for look you, the sins of the father are to be laid
upon the children. Therefore I promise you I fear you. I was
always plain with you, and so now I speak my agitation of the
matter. Therefore be o'good cheer, for truly I think you are
damned. There is but one hope in it that can do you any good, and   5
that is but a kind of bastard hope neither.

Jessica tells Lancelot that Lorenzo has converted her to Christianity.
Lorenzo accuses Lancelot of making a black girl pregnant. Lancelot doesn't
take it seriously.

1 Act out the scene (in groups of three)

Scene 5 is open to many interpretations. Prepare a performance or
reading for the class. Keep in mind:

- how the conversation began
- what Lancelot and Jessica are doing in this particular place (are
  they working together, or is Lancelot waiting upon Jessica at table?)
- what feelings Lancelot and Jessica have for one another
- how serious Lancelot is in his taunting of Jessica
- whether Lorenzo really is jealous of Lancelot
- why Lancelot's relationship with 'the Moor' is mentioned now
- whether Lancelot hides his intelligence and feelings behind a mask
  of clowning
- the balance between seriousness and playfulness
- whether you wish the audience to feel deeply sympathetic towards
  these three characters at this moment.

You will find that the scene makes a fascinating human triangle. Your
work will come over best if it includes movement and gesture.

2 Lancelot and 'the Moor'
(on your own or in groups of two or three)

It seems that Lancelot has made a black girl pregnant. Either as the
girl (or as her father) write a letter to Bassanio complaining about his
servant's irresponsible behaviour; or, act out the scene where the girl
or her father goes to visit Bassanio.

Scylla a legendary sea monster
Charybdis a legendary whirlpool
(the modern equivalent of
Lancelot's dilemma is 'between the
devil and the deep blue sea')

enow enough
e'en even
are out are arguing

JESSICA And what hope is that, I pray thee?

LANCELOT Marry, you may partly hope that your father got you not,
that you are not the Jew's daughter.

JESSICA That were a kind of bastard hope indeed; so the sins of my   10
mother should be visited upon me.

LANCELOT Truly, then, I fear you are damned both by father and
mother; thus when I shun Scylla your father, I fall into Charybdis
your mother. Well, you are gone both ways.

JESSICA I shall be saved by my husband; he hath made me a Christian.   15

LANCELOT Truly, the more to blame he; we were Christians enow
before, e'en as many as could well live one by another. This making
of Christians will raise the price of hogs; if we grow all to be pork
eaters, we shall not shortly have a rasher on the coals for
money.   20

Enter LORENZO

JESSICA I'll tell my husband, Lancelot, what you say: here he
comes.

LORENZO I shall grow jealous of you shortly, Lancelot, if you thus get
my wife into corners.

JESSICA Nay, you need not fear us, Lorenzo: Lancelot and I are out.   25
He tells me flatly there's no mercy for me in heaven, because I am
a Jew's daughter; and he says you are no good member of the
commonwealth, for in converting Jews to Christians you raise the
price of pork.

LORENZO I shall answer that better to the commonwealth than you can   30
the getting up of the Negro's belly: the Moor is with child by you,
Lancelot.

LANCELOT It is much that the Moor should be more than reason; but
if she be less than an honest woman, she is indeed more than I took
her for.   35

LORENZO How every fool can play upon the word! I think the best
grace of wit will shortly turn into silence, and discourse grow
commendable in none only but parrots. Go in, sirrah, bid them
prepare for dinner.

LANCELOT That is done, sir; they have all stomachs.   40

Lancelot deliberately misinterprets Lorenzo's words, but is sent off to arrange the serving of dinner. Jessica tells her husband how much she admires Portia. Lorenzo says he also has similar admirable qualities.

1 Prose and poetry (in pairs)

After Lancelot's exit, Lorenzo and Jessica speak in verse, not prose. Read lines 53–71 aloud to each other, then talk about why you think they are written as verse rather than prose.

2 Jessica: Portia's biggest fan? (in groups of three or four)

Jessica appears to be a huge admirer of 'Lord Bassanio's wife'. Notice that Lorenzo does not use Portia's name now that she is married to his friend. Jessica's speech is full of glowing compliments about Portia, yet she may have little reason to like or respect her. Talk together about:

- whether Portia deserves Jessica's praise
- why you think Shakespeare includes this tribute at this point in the play
- what image is created in lines 67–71. 'Pawned' means 'staked' or 'wagered'. Do you think the image is sexist? When you have talked about this, try drawing your version of the image!

3 Table-talk (in pairs)

As the two young lovers go in to dinner, Lorenzo comments that he is as admirable as Portia. Is he joking, or is he (as one production presented him) a humourless, pompous prig who treats his wife like a small child? Try both readings.

Jessica tells us that she will give her opinion of her husband later. Improvise the conversation that takes place over dinner when Jessica and Lorenzo share their impressions with each other.

---

cover lay the table (but Lancelot pretends it means 'put your hat on')
humours and conceits feelings and thoughts
O dear discretion . . . suited what nit-picking, how he twists his words

planted drawn up ready to fire
A many how many
tricksy ambiguous
Defy the matter will not speak plainly
meet fitting
rude primitive

LORENZO Goodly Lord, what a witsnapper are you! Then bid them
 prepare dinner.

LANCELOT That is done too, sir; only 'cover' is the word.

LORENZO Will you cover then, sir?

LANCELOT Not so, sir, neither; I know my duty.   45

LORENZO Yet more quarrelling with occasion! Wilt thou show the
 whole wealth of thy wit in an instant? I pray thee understand a
 plain man in his plain meaning: go to thy fellows, bid them cover
 the table, serve in the meat, and we will come in to dinner.

LANCELOT For the table, sir, it shall be served in; for the meat, sir, it   50
 shall be covered; for your coming in to dinner, sir, why, let it be as
 humours and conceits shall govern.   *Exit*

LORENZO O dear discretion, how his words are suited!
 The fool hath planted in his memory
 An army of good words; and I do know   55
 A many fools that stand in better place,
 Garnished like him, that for a tricksy word
 Defy the matter. How cheer'st thou, Jessica?
 And now, good sweet, say thy opinion:
 How dost thou like the Lord Bassanio's wife?   60

JESSICA Past all expressing. It is very meet
 The Lord Bassanio live an upright life,
 For having such a blessing in his lady
 He finds the joys of heaven here on earth,
 And if on earth he do not merit it,   65
 In reason he should never come to heaven.
 Why, if two gods should play some heavenly match,
 And on the wager lay two earthly women,
 And Portia one, there must be something else
 Pawned with the other, for the poor rude world   70
 Hath not her fellow.

LORENZO   Even such a husband
 Hast thou of me, as she is for a wife.

JESSICA Nay, but ask my opinion too of that.

LORENZO I will anon; first let us go to dinner.

JESSICA Nay, let me praise you while I have a stomach.   75

LORENZO No, pray thee, let it serve for table talk;
 Then howsome'er thou speak'st, 'mong other things
 I shall digest it.

JESSICA   Well, I'll set you forth.
                                            Exeunt

Looking back at Act 3
Activities for groups or individuals

1 The Rialto: what's it like?

The Rialto is where the business of Venice is done and gossip is exchanged. How would you show the Rialto in a film version of the play? Write or draw your impressions (see also page 28).

2 Design a 'Wanted' poster

In Scene 1 Shylock orders Antonio's arrest. Design the 'Wanted' poster which might be pasted up around Venice. Give details of Antonio's 'crime' and probable punishment. Remember: Shylock is likely to write the poster's contents himself.

3 Shylock's repetitions

In Scene 1 Shylock often repeats certain words. Make a list of his repetitions. Decide why these words are of such importance to him. What is the dramatic effect of Shylock speaking in this way?

4 The most important lines?

'The villainy you teach me I will execute, and it shall go hard but I will better the instruction.' (3.1.56–7)

The director Sir Peter Hall described these lines as the most important in the play, because they show Shakespeare's understanding of why Shylock behaves so harshly. Talk together about whether you agree with this view.

5 Lorenzo and Jessica go wild

In Scene 1 Tubal reports on the young runaways' spending spree. Improvise a short scene showing Lorenzo and Jessica's behaviour in Genoa.

6 Dip for a duchess!

Once again, you are the gossip columnist for the *Belmont Gazette* (see page 66). Follow up your article on Arragon's courtship of Portia with one about Bassanio's choosing between the caskets.

7 First words . . .

Read aloud the first four lines of each scene. Do this a few times, then talk together about the differences between the language of each. How far do these 'openings' set the mood of each scene?

8 Why does Shylock hate Antonio?

'I oft delivered from his forfeitures/Many that have at times made moan to me' (3.3.22–3) is Antonio's explanation for Shylock's hatred of him. Shylock probably has other reasons for his hatred. Make a full list of Shylock's reasons for hating Antonio. Give short quotations from the script as an example of each reason.

9 'The Duke cannot deny the course of law!' (3.3.31–6)

Antonio seems to see himself as a victim of trade and politics: it will damage the business reputation of Venice if the Duke does not allow Shylock his legal rights over Antonio. Talk together about:

- how much Antonio is personally to blame for his plight
- how much he is the victim of Shylock's personal animosity
- how much he is a victim of a society that values trade over human life.

Can you think of any contemporary figures who have gambled in business and either lost or gained everything? Do you see them as villains or heroes?

10 Keeping Belmont in mind

What impressions of Belmont have you acquired so far in the play? Copy out the example below and complete ten contrasting sentences for the two locations, Venice and Belmont:

Belmont is _____; Venice is _____ .

11 Five scenes: five words

Catch the essence of each scene in Act 3 in a single word. Compare your five words with other students' lists.

12 Jessica, from Portia's viewpoint

What does Portia think of Jessica? Write a speech for Portia (in iambic pentameter, if possible) in which she gives her impression of Jessica.

The Duke's court assembles to judge Shylock's case against Antonio. The Duke sympathises with Antonio, and tells Shylock that he expects him to show mercy at the last moment.

1 The whole scene (in groups of no more than eight)

Gain a first impression of this famous trial. Take parts and read the whole scene through. (Parts: The Duke, Antonio, Salerio, Bassanio, Gratiano, Shylock, Nerissa and Portia)

2 Set the trial scene (in pairs)

Where is the trial to be held? Talk together about possibilities, then sketch a set design.

3 Enter the Duke and Shylock (in large groups)

Use the stage direction to allocate parts. Work out how to stage the Duke's entrance. Remember he was a world-famous figure, and great ceremony accompanied all his appearances. Then stage Shylock's entrance. How will he be received in a court full of Christians?

4 Shylock: what's he thinking?

Shylock is 'ready at the door' (line 15). Imagine that Shakespeare has written a soliloquy for him in which he reveals his true feelings to the audience. Write your own version of Shylock's soliloquy, expressing his feelings at this dramatic moment in the play. He is about to enter a room full of enemies, but might be only minutes from gaining his much-desired revenge.

---

adversary opponent
dram drop
tane taken
obdurate stubborn
envy's hatred's
thou . . . act you will keep up this pretence only until the last moment

remorse pity
loose cancel
Forgive . . . principal ask for repayment of only some of the loan
enow enough

ACT 4 SCENE 1
The Duke's palace in Venice

Enter the DUKE, *the Magnificoes,* ANTONIO, BASSANIO, SALERIO, *and* GRATIANO, *with others*

DUKE What, is Antonio here?

ANTONIO Ready, so please your grace.

DUKE I am sorry for thee. Thou art come to answer
    A stony adversary, an inhuman wretch,
    Uncapable of pity, void and empty   5
    From any dram of mercy.

ANTONIO   I have heard
    Your grace hath tane great pains to qualify
    His rigorous course; but since he stands obdùrate
    And that no lawful means can carry me
    Out of his envy's reach, I do oppose   10
    My patience to his fury, and am armed
    To suffer with a quietness of spirit
    The very tyranny and rage of his.

DUKE Go one and call the Jew into the court.

SALERIO He is ready at the door; he comes, my lord.   15

Enter SHYLOCK

DUKE Make room and let him stand before our face.
    Shylock, the world thinks, and I think so too,
    That thou but lead'st this fashion of thy malice
    To the last hour of act, and then 'tis thought
    Thou'lt show thy mercy and remorse more strange   20
    Than is thy strange apparent cruelty.
    And where thou now exacts the penalty,
    Which is a pound of this poor merchant's flesh,
    Thou wilt not only loose the forfeiture
    But, touched with human gentleness and love,   25
    Forgive a moiety of the principal,
    Glancing an eye of pity on his losses
    That have of late so huddled on his back,
    Enow to press a royal merchant down

The Duke asks Shylock to show pity. Shylock refuses to give his reasons for wishing to harm Antonio, except that it is his whim, and that he hates him.

1 The Duke: first impressions (in groups of five or six)

Try a group reading of lines 16–34, sharing the lines between you. Look out for clues to the Duke's feelings for Antonio and his attitudes to non-Christians. Talk together about whether it is possible for the Duke to give Shylock a fair hearing.

2 Shylock's curse

Shylock is determined to use the Venetian code of law to press his case against Antonio. If the Duke will not enforce the law, then 'the danger' will result (lines 38–9). Write a paragraph or draw a picture to show what Shylock wishes might happen to 'your charter and your city's freedom' if the law is not followed.

3 Women's fears (in pairs)

In lines 47–52 Shylock lists three things which some men find disturbing or hateful. As usual, it's the male point of view. Make up a similar list of what women find frightening or loathsome. As you compile your list, talk together about whether men and women really do have different fears.

4 Shylock won't explain (in pairs)

Share reading aloud lines 35–62. Change over at the end of each line or at each punctuation mark. Earlier in the play (page 21) Shylock publicly described his grievances against Antonio; yet now, in the court, he refuses to discuss his feelings, except publicly to confirm his hatred for Antonio. Talk together about possible reasons for Shylock's behaviour at this vital point in his revenge plan.

And pluck . . . flint and make even the most hard-hearted feel sorry for him
Turks and Tartars seen by Christians as heathens (like the Jews)

baned poisoned
affection . . . passion strong feelings often disturb the mind
but of . . . offended but can't help offending others because he himself is so offended

And pluck commiseration of his state   30
From brassy bosoms and rough hearts of flint,
From stubborn Turks, and Tartars never trained
To offices of tender courtesy.
We all expect a gentle answer, Jew.
SHYLOCK I have possessed your grace of what I purpose,   35
And by our holy Sabaoth have I sworn
To have the due and forfeit of my bond.
If you deny it, let the danger light
Upon your charter and your city's freedom!
You'll ask me why I rather choose to have   40
A weight of carrion flesh than to receive
Three thousand ducats. I'll not answer that –
But say it is my humour: is it answered?
What if my house be troubled with a rat,
And I be pleased to give ten thousand ducats   45
To have it baned? What, are you answered yet?
Some men there are love not a gaping pig;
Some that are mad if they behold a cat;
And others when the bagpipe sings i'the nose
Cannot contain their urine: for affection   50
Masters oft passion, sways it to the mood
Of what it likes or loathes. Now for your answer:
As there is no firm reason to be rendered
Why he cannot abide a gaping pig,
Why he a harmless necessary cat,   55
Why he a woollen bagpipe, but of force
Must yield to such inevitable shame
As to offend, himself being offended:
So can I give no reason, nor I will not,
More than a lodged hate and a certain loathing   60
I bear Antonio, that I follow thus
A losing suit against him. Are you answered?
BASSANIO This is no answer, thou unfeeling man,
To excuse the current of thy cruelty.

Antonio says it's pointless to argue with the pitiless Shylock. Bassanio's offer of six thousand ducats is refused. Shylock demands the pound of flesh as his property, and due to him by law.

1 Shylock won't listen (in pairs)

In lines 70–83 Antonio stresses how immovable and stubborn Shylock is. Reasoning with him is like trying to stop the waves on the beach or the wolf from eating the lamb. Make up another futile task to add to Antonio's list. Mime it to the rest of the class. Can they tell what it is?

2 Give me judgement!

Lines 89–103 are Shylock's passionate plea for his case to be heard.

a Learn and prepare his speech for an audience. Bring out Shylock's vehemence and commitment.

b How does the Duke respond as he listens to Shylock's tirade against Venice? Work in pairs. One reads, pausing at the end of each sentence for the other, as the Duke, to speak his thoughts.

c Shylock claims to own Antonio's flesh in the same way as the Christians own slaves. His words (lines 89–103) give another glimpse of the lives of the underprivileged in Venice. In groups of three or four, talk together about what Shylock's words tell you about master–slave relationships. How does that knowledge add to your understanding of Venetian society?

Every ... first not all insults provoke hatred at first
bate reduce
fretten disturbed, blown about
moe more
brief and plain conveniency speed

rendering giving
palates mouths
viands food
fie upon so much for
decrees laws

SHYLOCK I am not bound to please thee with my answers.   65
BASSANIO Do all men kill the things they do not love?
SHYLOCK Hates any man the thing he would not kill?
BASSANIO Every offence is not a hate at first.
SHYLOCK What, wouldst thou have a serpent sting thee twice?
ANTONIO I pray you think you question with the Jew.   70
   You may as well go stand upon the beach
   And bid the main flood bate his usual height;
   You may as well use question with the wolf
   Why he hath made the ewe bleat for the lamb;
   You may as well forbid the mountain pines   75
   To wag their high tops and to make no noise
   When they are fretten with the gusts of heaven;
   You may as well do anything most hard
   As seek to soften that – than which what's harder? –
   His Jewish heart. Therefore I do beseech you   80
   Make no moe offers, use no farther means,
   But with all brief and plain conveniency
   Let me have judgement, and the Jew his will.
BASSANIO For thy three thousand ducats here is six.
SHYLOCK If every ducat in six thousand ducats   85
   Were in six parts, and every part a ducat,
   I would not draw them; I would have my bond.
DUKE How shalt thou hope for mercy, rendering none?
SHYLOCK What judgement shall I dread, doing no wrong?
   You have among you many a purchased slave,   90
   Which, like your asses and your dogs and mules,
   You use in abject and in slavish parts
   Because you bought them. Shall I say to you,
   'Let them be free! Marry them to your heirs!
   Why sweat they under burdens? Let their beds   95
   Be made as soft as yours, and let their palates
   Be seasoned with such viands'? You will answer,
   'The slaves are ours.' So do I answer you.
   The pound of flesh which I demand of him
   Is dearly bought; 'tis mine, and I will have it.   100
   If you deny me, fie upon your law:
   There is no force in the decrees of Venice.
   I stand for judgement. Answer: shall I have it?

Nerissa, disguised as a messenger, arrives from Bellario, a legal expert. Shylock sharpens his knife on the sole of his shoe, and Gratiano abuses him for his cruel nature.

1 Shylock sharpens his knife (in groups of five or six)

Choosing a character each, make your own tableau of the moment in court when Bassanio speaks line 121. Decide what you would be doing and thinking at this crucial moment. Show your image to the rest of the class. As you do so, take turns to speak your character's thoughts.

Which line do you think Shylock is speaking at this moment?

2 Gratiano attacks (in groups of five or six)

Gratiano viciously abuses Shylock, saying that a dead wolf's soul entered his body whilst he was still in his mother's womb. One person, as Shylock, sits on a chair. The others speak, shout or sneer lines 128–38 at him, changing over at each punctuation mark. Take turns to be Shylock. Afterwards, talk about how he must feel and what these words suggest about Gratiano.

determine settle
stays without waits outside
ere before
tainted wether sick ram
meetest the most suitable
epitaph words on a tomb or gravestone

keen sharp (or sing a funeral song)
wit intelligence
inexecrable utterly cursed
Pythagoras Greek who taught the transmigration of souls
trunks bodies
unhallowed dam heathen mother

DUKE Upon my power I may dismiss this court,
    Unless Bellario, a learned doctor   105
    Whom I have sent for to determine this,
    Come here today.
SALERIO   My lord, here stays without
    A messenger with letters from the doctor,
    New come from Padua.
DUKE Bring us the letters. Call the messenger.   110
BASSANIO Good cheer, Antonio! What, man, courage yet!
    The Jew shall have my flesh, blood, bones, and all,
    Ere thou shalt lose for me one drop of blood.
ANTONIO I am a tainted wether of the flock,
    Meetest for death; the weakest kind of fruit   115
    Drops earliest to the ground, and so let me.
    You cannot better be employed, Bassanio,
    Than to live still and write mine epitaph.

Enter NERISSA [*disguised as a lawyer's clerk*]

DUKE Came you from Padua, from Bellario?
NERISSA From both, my lord: [*Presenting letter*] Bellario greets your
        grace.   120
BASSANIO Why dost thou whet thy knife so earnestly?
SHYLOCK To cut the forfeiture from that bankrupt there.
GRATIANO Not on thy sole, but on thy soul, harsh Jew,
    Thou mak'st thy knife keen. But no metal can,
    No, not the hangman's axe, bear half the keenness   125
    Of thy sharp envy. Can no prayers pierce thee?
SHYLOCK No, none that thou hast wit enough to make.
GRATIANO O be thou damned, inexecrable dog,
    And for thy life let justice be accused!
    Thou almost mak'st me waver in my faith,   130
    To hold opinion with Pythagoras
    That souls of animals infuse themselves
    Into the trunks of men. Thy currish spirit
    Governed a wolf, who – hanged for human slaughter –
    Even from the gallows did his fell soul fleet,   135
    And whilst thou layest in thy unhallowed dam
    Infused itself in thee; for thy desires
    Are wolfish, bloody, starved, and ravenous.

Bellario's letter is read out. He is ill, but has sent Doctor Balthazar in his place. Portia enters in disguise as Balthazar and announces that she is fully informed of the case.

1 The Duke's letter

We learn from Bellario (line 150) that the Duke had contacted him by letter to request his assistance with this difficult and embarrassing case. Write your version of the Duke's letter.

2 Bellario's letter: point out who's involved
(in groups of six)

Take a part each (Bellario, Balthazar, Antonio, Shylock, the Duke, Duke's messenger). Stand in a circle. Bellario reads the letter, slowly. Everyone points to whoever is mentioned in any way (for example, *'your grace'*, 'I', 'your', and so on). Afterwards, talk together about how this activity helps your understanding.

3 Balthazar: a legal whiz kid

The letter is part of Portia's disguise. It pays 'Balthazar' many compliments. Pick out the words and phrases about him which are intended to impress the court. Think about why Portia wants these to be heard before she enters the courtroom.

4 A woman takes on the men

Venice is a male-dominated society: business and the law are for men alone. But now Portia is about to challenge the men at their own game. What is she thinking as she waits outside? Write her thoughts as she awaits the moment when she will be summoned to appear in the male world of the court.

---

rail abuse, revile
wit intelligence
loving visitation friendly visit
furnished provided
importunity pressing request
stead place

I beseech . . . estimation Take my advice: don't let his youth stop you from respecting him
whose . . . commendation the trial will improve his reputation
difference dispute

SHYLOCK Till thou canst rail the seal from off my bond
　　　　Thou but offend'st thy lungs to speak so loud.　　　140
　　　　Repair thy wit, good youth, or it will fall
　　　　To cureless ruin. I stand here for law.
DUKE This letter from Bellario doth commend
　　　　A young and learned doctor to our court:
　　　　Where is he?
NERISSA　　　　　　He attendeth here hard by　　　145
　　　　To know your answer whether you'll admit him.
DUKE With all my heart. Some three or four of you
　　　　Go give him courteous conduct to this place.
　　　　　　　　　　　　　　　　　[Exeunt officials]
　　　　Meantime the court shall hear Bellario's letter.
[Reads] 'Your grace shall understand, that at the receipt of your letter　150
　　　　I am very sick; but in the instant that your messenger came, in
　　　　loving visitation was with me a young doctor of Rome: his name
　　　　is Balthazar. I acquainted him with the cause in controversy
　　　　between the Jew and Antonio the merchant. We turned o'er many
　　　　books together; he is furnished with my opinion which, bettered　155
　　　　with his own learning, the greatness whereof I cannot enough
　　　　commend, comes with him at my importunity, to fill up your
　　　　grace's request in my stead. I beseech you let his lack of years be
　　　　no impediment to let him lack a reverend estimation, for I never
　　　　knew so young a body with so old a head. I leave him to your　160
　　　　gracious acceptance, whose trial shall better publish his com-
　　　　mendation.'

　　　Enter PORTIA [disguised as Doctor Balthazar, followed by officials]

　　　　You hear the learn'd Bellario what he writes,
　　　　And here I take it is the doctor come.
　　　　Give me your hand. Come you from old Bellario?　　165
PORTIA I did, my lord.
DUKE　　　　　　　　You are welcome; take your place.
　　　　Are you acquainted with the difference
　　　　That holds this present question in the court?
PORTIA I am informèd throughly of the cause.
　　　　Which is the merchant here and which the Jew?　　170

Portia appeals unsuccessfully to Shylock to show mercy. She explains that mercy can be neither forced nor diluted, and is greater than any monarch's power. Mercy and justice should go hand in hand, for mercy, not justice, will save us.

1 'The quality of mercy'

Portia's speech is world-famous. Try some of the following activities to help you understand its powerful appeal to women and men in all ages and all cultures.

- Stand in a circle. Take turns to read aloud lines 180–93, handing over at each punctuation mark. Now read it again, but this time each reader adds a mime to illustrate the language. The whole group should repeat each reader's words and actions.
- Discuss whether, in line 193, Portia is openly anti-Semitic.
- Find the Cambridge School Shakespeare *Measure for Measure* and read its Act 2 Scene 2, lines 59–67 alongside Portia's speech. What do the two speeches have in common? Can you interweave them for dramatic effect?
- Organise your own class debate about the conflict between justice and mercy. Should those who were guilty of the Holocaust have been shown mercy or justice? Would you follow Portia's advice and show mercy as well as justice to the Nazi soldier in this photograph?

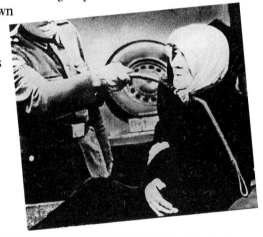

---

impugn oppose
becomes suits
temporal earthly
attribute to quality of
sceptred sway the authority of a
  monarch

seasons blends with
salvation life after death in heaven
render . . . mercy behave
  mercifully
mitigate moderate or tone down

DUKE Antonio and old Shylock, both stand forth.
PORTIA Is your name Shylock?
SHYLOCK   Shylock is my name.
PORTIA Of a strange nature is the suit you follow,
        Yet in such rule that the Venetian law
        Cannot impugn you as you do proceed.   175
        – You stand within his danger, do you not?
ANTONIO Ay, so he says.
PORTIA   Do you confess the bond?
ANTONIO I do.
PORTIA   Then must the Jew be merciful.
SHYLOCK On what compulsion must I? Tell me that.
PORTIA The quality of mercy is not strained,   180
        It droppeth as the gentle rain from heaven
        Upon the place beneath. It is twice blest:
        It blesseth him that gives, and him that takes.
        'Tis mightiest in the mightiest, it becomes
        The thronèd monarch better than his crown.   185
        His sceptre shows the force of temporal power,
        The attribute to awe and majesty,
        Wherein doth sit the dread and fear of kings;
        But mercy is above this sceptred sway.
        It is enthronèd in the hearts of kings,   190
        It is an attribute to God himself,
        And earthly power doth then show likest God's
        When mercy seasons justice. Therefore, Jew,
        Though justice be thy plea, consider this:
        That in the course of justice, none of us   195
        Should see salvation. We do pray for mercy,
        And that same prayer doth teach us all to render
        The deeds of mercy. I have spoke thus much
        To mitigate the justice of thy plea,
        Which if thou follow, this strict court of Venice   200
        Must needs give sentence 'gainst the merchant there.

Bassanio asks Portia to bend the law to save Antonio, but she refuses, as other legal cases would be affected. Despite offers of trebled payment, Shylock implacably refuses to give way.

1 Doesn't her husband recognise her? (in pairs)

Portia and Bassanio actually have a conversation, yet he does not see through her disguise. Work together on their exchange and decide how Portia's appearance, tone of voice and movement can make Bassanio's lack of recognition seem credible.

2 Right to do wrong? (in small groups)

'To do a great right, do a little wrong' (line 212) says Bassanio. Has he got a point? Would you do wrong if you thought it would result in good? Talk together, giving examples.

3 Portia: appearance and reality (in pairs and everyone)

Read lines 219–52, noting what Shylock says about Balthazar (Portia). Then prepare two tableaux: one showing Shylock's opinion of Portia, the other revealing her true personality. Share your work with the class, and talk about how Portia's deception of Shylock might affect the audience's attitude to him.

4 Antonio at breaking point?

The pressure Antonio is under emerges in lines 239–40. He has said little since Portia entered the court, but what has he been thinking? Write his varying reactions to all that is said opposite. Show how his thoughts culminate in his urgent plea for a quick decision.

My deeds ... head I'll take responsibility for my own actions
crave demand
malice evil
wrest ... authority use your power to change the law
curb deprive
precedent a case to be used as an example

'Twill ... state Many other cases will be mistakenly based on this one as a precedent
Daniel Jewish prophet known for catching out liars
perjury lying under oath
tenour small print
exposition explanation

SHYLOCK My deeds upon my head! I crave the law,
　　　　The penalty and forfeit of my bond.
PORTIA Is he not able to discharge the money?
BASSANIO Yes, here I tender it for him in the court,　　　　205
　　　　Yea, twice the sum; if that will not suffice,
　　　　I will be bound to pay it ten times o'er
　　　　On forfeit of my hands, my head, my heart.
　　　　If this will not suffice, it must appear
　　　　That malice bears down truth. And I beseech you　　　　210
　　　　Wrest once the law to your authority;
　　　　To do a great right, do a little wrong,
　　　　And curb this cruel devil of his will.
PORTIA It must not be; there is no power in Venice
　　　　Can alter a decree establishèd.　　　　215
　　　　'Twill be recorded for a precedent,
　　　　And many an error by the same example
　　　　Will rush into the state: it cannot be.
SHYLOCK A Daniel come to judgement; yea a Daniel!
　　　　O wise young judge, how I do honour thee!　　　　220
PORTIA I pray you let me look upon the bond.
SHYLOCK Here 'tis, most reverend doctor, here it is.
PORTIA Shylock, there's thrice thy money offered thee.
SHYLOCK An oath, an oath. I have an oath in heaven!
　　　　Shall I lay perjury upon my soul?　　　　225
　　　　No, not for Venice.
PORTIA　　　　　　　　　　Why, this bond is forfeit,
　　　　And lawfully by this the Jew may claim
　　　　A pound of flesh, to be by him cut off
　　　　Nearest the merchant's heart. Be merciful:
　　　　Take thrice thy money; bid me tear the bond.　　　　230
SHYLOCK When it is paid, according to the tenour.
　　　　It doth appear you are a worthy judge,
　　　　You know the law, your exposition
　　　　Hath been most sound. I charge you by the law,
　　　　Whereof you are a well-deserving pillar,　　　　235
　　　　Proceed to judgement. By my soul I swear
　　　　There is no power in the tongue of man
　　　　To alter me. I stay here on my bond.
ANTONIO Most heartily I do beseech the court
　　　　To give the judgement.

Portia judges that Shylock must have his pound of flesh. Antonio is now prepared to die. He lovingly bids farewell to Bassanio, saying that he is glad to be spared a life of poverty.

1 Add the stage directions (in pairs)

There are no stage directions for this page, but it is clear from the script that a great deal is happening. Make a list (with line numbers) of the movements and gestures you would enact in lines 240–60.

2 The surgeon

As a bystander in the court, write a paragraph giving your reactions to the conversation about the surgeon in lines 253–8. What do you see and hear, and how do you feel about it?

3 Antonio's last words to Bassanio? (in pairs)

Work together on how you think the two actors should handle lines 260–77. Experiment with different versions. Decide how Antonio speaks and moves, and how Bassanio reacts to his words.

4 A life without wealth

Antonio dreads a life of poverty more than death itself. Draw a picture to represent the feelings he expresses in lines 266–7.

intent and purpose meaning and
  intention
Hath ... to fully authorises
balance scales
armed ready
Fortune fate

is her custom usual
use habit
speak ... death speak well of me
  when I'm gone
Repent but you just feel sorry

PORTIA   Why then, thus it is: 240
    You must prepare your bosom for his knife.
SHYLOCK O noble judge, O excellent young man!
PORTIA For the intent and purpose of the law
    Hath full relation to the penalty
    Which here appeareth due upon the bond.   245
SHYLOCK 'Tis very true. O wise and upright judge,
    How much more elder art thou than thy looks!
PORTIA Therefore lay bare your bosom.
SHYLOCK   Ay, his breast.
    So says the bond, doth it not, noble judge?
    'Nearest his heart': those are the very words.   250
PORTIA It is so. Are there balance here to weigh
    The flesh?
SHYLOCK   I have them ready.
PORTIA Have by some surgeon, Shylock, on your charge,
    To stop his wounds, lest he do bleed to death.
SHYLOCK Is it so nominated in the bond?   255
PORTIA It is not so expressed, but what of that?
    'Twere good you do so much for charity.
SHYLOCK I cannot find it, 'tis not in the bond.
PORTIA You, merchant: have you anything to say?
ANTONIO But little; I am armed and well prepared.   260
    Give me your hand, Bassanio. Fare you well.
    Grieve not that I am fall'n to this for you.
    For herein Fortune shows herself more kind
    Than is her custom: it is still her use
    To let the wretched man outlive his wealth,   265
    To view with hollow eye and wrinkled brow
    An age of poverty; from which ling'ring penance
    Of such misery doth she cut me off.
    Commend me to your honourable wife.
    Tell her the process of Antonio's end,   270
    Say how I loved you, speak me fair in death,
    And when the tale is told, bid her be judge
    Whether Bassanio had not once a love.
    Repent but you that you shall lose your friend
    And he repents not that he pays your debt.   275
    For if the Jew do cut but deep enough
    I'll pay it instantly with all my heart.

Portia gives judgement in Shylock's favour but, at the last moment, saves Antonio. Blood is not mentioned in the bond, so Shylock must break the law if he sheds Antonio's.

1 They wish their wives were dead! (in groups of four)

Both Bassanio (lines 278–83) and Gratiano (lines 286–8) would sacrifice their wives for Antonio. The audience knows (but the two men don't) that Portia and Nerissa are listening. In the middle of what looks like a tragic scene, Shakespeare lightens the mood. Talk about how he uses Portia's and Nerissa's disguises to humorous effect, and why he changes the emotional balance of the scene at this point.

If this picture were to appear in a teenage magazine photo-story version of *The Merchant of Venice*, what would the caption be?

2 Portia's coup ... 'Tarry a little' (in pairs)

Portia must have known all along about this loophole in Shylock's bond. Share a reading of lines 294–300, bringing out the game of cat and mouse which Portia is obviously playing with Shylock. Then concentrate on lines 301–8. Work on how the words should be spoken, and how Shylock should react. How near is Shylock to cutting Antonio when Portia stops him?

---

esteemed valued
currish dog-like
else otherwise
stock family
Barabbas a Jewish thief pardoned
  by Pontius Pilate instead of Jesus

trifle waste
tarry wait
urgest demand

BASSANIO Antonio, I am married to a wife
    Which is as dear to me as life itself;
    But life itself, my wife, and all the world,   280
    Are not with me esteemed above thy life.
    I would lose all, ay, sacrifice them all
    Here to this devil, to deliver you.
PORTIA Your wife would give you little thanks for that
    If she were by to hear you make the offer.   285
GRATIANO I have a wife who I protest I love;
    I would she were in heaven, so she could
    Entreat some power to change this currish Jew.
NERISSA 'Tis well you offer it behind her back;
    The wish would make else an unquiet house.   290
SHYLOCK These be the Christian husbands! I have a daughter:
    Would any of the stock of Barabbas
    Had been her husband, rather than a Christian!
    We trifle time; I pray thee pursue sentence.
PORTIA A pound of that same merchant's flesh is thine,   295
    The court awards it, and the law doth give it.
SHYLOCK Most rightful judge!
PORTIA And you must cut this flesh from off his breast;
    The law allows it, and the court awards it.
SHYLOCK Most learned judge! A sentence: come, prepare.   300
PORTIA Tarry a little, there is something else.
    This bond doth give thee here no jot of blood.
    The words expressly are 'a pound of flesh'.
    Take then thy bond, take thou thy pound of flesh,
    But in the cutting it, if thou dost shed   305
    One drop of Christian blood, thy lands and goods
    Are by the laws of Venice confiscate
    Unto the state of Venice.
GRATIANO   O upright judge!
    Mark, Jew – O learned judge!
SHYLOCK Is that the law?
PORTIA   Thyself shall see the Act.   310
    For as thou urgest justice, be assured
    Thou shalt have justice more than thou desirest.

Shylock is defeated, and Portia insists on justice. She will not allow him to be repaid any money, only to take the pound of flesh at his peril.

---

1 Portia in control (in groups of four to six)

Shylock, sensing that victory is slipping away, agrees to accept a financial settlement of his bond. Bassanio is prepared to hand over the money, but Portia insists that 'justice' must prevail and that Shylock must exact the penalty. She shows that she is more than equal to the men of Venice.

- Read over Portia's speeches on the opposite page. Work out gestures you could use to accompany each statement she makes.
- Choose three quotations to show that Portia is in charge of events.
- Talk about whether you admire her assertiveness. Women have little freedom in Venice, but is she setting a good example to other women in her treatment of Shylock?

2 Peripeteia: a reversal of fortune (in pairs)

A few moments ago Shylock seemed triumphant, but now Portia has turned the tables on him. She is determined to punish him for his treatment of Antonio. Read aloud only Shylock's words from line 294 to line 342, and trace the stages of his decline and loss of dignity.

3 'I have you on the hip'

Gratiano is pleased to use Shylock's own words against him (line 330). Look back to Act 1 Scene 3 to find Shylock's original use of this expression. Decide on a gesture to go with Gratiano's taunt – for example, does he refer to where Shylock keeps his purse?

---

thrice three times over
soft not so fast
penalty the pound of flesh
As makes . . . scruple even if it's just by a fraction
scruple gram

principal the original sum owed (3,000 ducats)
the devil . . . it he's welcome to it
I'll stay . . . question I'm not staying to argue about this

GRATIANO O learned judge! Mark, Jew: a learned judge.

SHYLOCK I take this offer then. Pay the bond thrice
>And let the Christian go.

BASSANIO   Here is the money.   315

PORTIA Soft.
>The Jew shall have all justice; soft, no haste;
>He shall have nothing but the penalty.

GRATIANO O Jew, an upright judge, a learned judge!

PORTIA Therefore prepare thee to cut off the flesh.   320
>Shed thou no blood, nor cut thou less nor more
>But just a pound of flesh. If thou tak'st more
>Or less than a just pound, be it but so much
>As makes it light or heavy in the substance
>Or the division of the twentieth part   325
>Of one poor scruple – nay, if the scale do turn
>But in the estimation of a hair,
>Thou diest, and all thy goods are confiscate.

GRATIANO A second Daniel; a Daniel, Jew!
>Now, infidel, I have you on the hip.   330

PORTIA Why doth the Jew pause? Take thy forfeiture.

SHYLOCK Give me my principal, and let me go.

BASSANIO I have it ready for thee; here it is.

PORTIA He hath refused it in the open court.
>He shall have merely justice and his bond.   335

GRATIANO A Daniel, still say I, a second Daniel!
>I thank thee, Jew, for teaching me that word.

SHYLOCK Shall I not have barely my principal?

PORTIA Thou shalt have nothing but the forfeiture,
>To be so taken at thy peril, Jew.   340

SHYLOCK Why then, the devil give him good of it!
>I'll stay no longer question.

Portia reveals another trap for Shylock. If a foreigner plots to kill a Venetian, the punishment by law should be confiscation of all wealth, and possible execution.

1 Portia's legal language

Portia's words (lines 342–59) sound almost as if she is reading from the laws of Venice. Re-write her speech in your own words, as if you are having to explain to a friend the details of how Shylock has broken the law and how he might be punished.

2 Is the law fair? (in pairs)

Improvise an argument about the law Shylock has broken. One should be a native Venetian, the other a member of a non-Christian group living in Venice. How does an 'alien' feel about such possible treatment at the hands of the law? How can a Venetian justify such legal prejudice?

3 Gratiano the persecutor (in pairs)

Shylock is ordered by Portia to kneel to the Duke and plead for mercy. But Gratiano again abuses Shylock. Take turns to be Gratiano and Shylock. Experiment with how lines 360–3 might be spoken. Try the words in as many different ways as possible, and talk about the effects you achieve.

4 Is this the final blow? (in groups of four or five)

Shylock is devastated by the loss of his wealth. Devise a mime or tableau to represent the anguish expressed in lines 371–3.

---

enacted stated
alien foreigner
The party . . . contrive the person who is plotted against
privy coffer the Duke's personal fortune
'gainst all other voice without appeal
by manifest proceeding obvious

danger . . . rehearsed the punishments I've just explained
leave permission
spirit natures
house . . . house you destroy my family when you remove my means of supporting my home
halter gratis a free hangman's noose

PORTIA   Tarry, Jew:
          The law hath yet another hold on you.
          It is enacted in the laws of Venice,
          If it be proved against an alien   345
          That by direct or indirect attempts
          He seek the life of any citizen,
          The party 'gainst the which he doth contrive
          Shall seize one half his goods, the other half
          Comes to the privy coffer of the state,   350
          And the offender's life lies in the mercy
          Of the Duke only, 'gainst all other voice.
          In which predicament I say thou stand'st;
          For it appears by manifest proceeding
          That indirectly, and directly too,   355
          Thou hast contrived against the very life
          Of the defendant, and thou hast incurred
          The danger formerly by me rehearsed.
          Down, therefore, and beg mercy of the Duke.
GRATIANO Beg that thou mayst have leave to hang thyself –   360
          And yet, thy wealth being forfeit to the state,
          Thou hast not left the value of a cord;
          Therefore thou must be hanged at the state's charge.
DUKE That thou shalt see the difference of our spirit,
          I pardon thee thy life before thou ask it.   365
          For half thy wealth, it is Antonio's;
          The other half comes to the general state,
          Which humbleness may drive unto a fine.
PORTIA Ay, for the state, not for Antonio.
SHYLOCK Nay, take my life and all, pardon not that: 370
          You take my house when you do take the prop
          That doth sustain my house; you take my life
          When you do take the means whereby I live.
PORTIA What mercy can you render him, Antonio?
GRATIANO A halter gratis – nothing else, for God's sake.   375

*Antonio requests – and is granted – partial mercy for Shylock: he can keep
half his wealth; Antonio will invest the rest. Unwittingly, Bassanio
tries to reward Portia with her own money.*

---

1 Shylock's punishment: a summary (in pairs)

Use lines 376–86 to make a diagram, illustrating in words and
pictures Antonio's suggestions for the punishment of Shylock. Find a
clear way of showing the order in which they might rank in Shylock's
mind in humiliating him.

2 Antonio: a merciful Christian? (in small groups)

Talk together about Antonio's treatment of Shylock. Has he given up
the vicious prejudice of his past, or are these reduced punishments
(lines 376–86) still calculated to inflict misery and humiliation on
Shylock? In particular, discuss the demand that Shylock becomes a
Christian.

3 Shylock's last lines (in pairs)

A director said that Shylock should speak his last lines 'with all the
ruefulness of a man who realises he's made a very silly mistake . . . to
take on the establishment and play it at its own game . . .' This is only
one opinion. There are plenty of other ways to play it. Experiment
with how lines 389 and 391–3 should be delivered.

4 Exit Shylock

Shakespeare gives Shylock virtually nothing to say before he leaves.
How, then, can his final exit be used to make one last statement to the
audience? (For example, Laurence Olivier as Shylock made his exit in
a dignified manner, but after he'd gone off, a long, agonised scream
was heard.) As director, write instructions for Shylock about how he
should leave the stage.

---

have . . . use invest the other half
record a gift sign a deed of gift
of all . . . possessed everything he
  owns when he dies
had . . . more if I'd had my way,
  you'd have been in front of a jury

meet necessary
leisure time
gratify reward
bond in debt
in lieu in place of
cope give in exchange for

ANTONIO So please my lord the Duke and all the court
　　　　To quit the fine for one half of his goods,
　　　　I am content, so he will let me have
　　　　The other half in use, to render it
　　　　Upon his death unto the gentleman　　　　　　380
　　　　That lately stole his daughter.
　　　　Two things provided more: that for this favour
　　　　He presently become a Christian;
　　　　The other, that he do record a gift,
　　　　Here in the court, of all he dies possessed　　385
　　　　Unto his son Lorenzo and his daughter.
DUKE He shall do this, or else I do recant
　　　　The pardon that I late pronouncèd here.
PORTIA Art thou contented, Jew? What dost thou say?
SHYLOCK I am content.
PORTIA　　　　　　　　Clerk, draw a deed of gift.　　390
SHYLOCK I pray you give me leave to go from hence;
　　　　I am not well. Send the deed after me
　　　　And I will sign it.
DUKE　　　　　　　　Get thee gone, but do it.
GRATIANO In christening shalt thou have two godfathers:
　　　　Had I been judge, thou shouldst have had ten more,　　395
　　　　To bring thee to the gallows, not to the font.
　　　　　　　　　　　　　　　　Exit [Shylock]
DUKE Sir, I entreat you home with me to dinner.
PORTIA I humbly do desire your grace of pardon.
　　　　I must away this night toward Padua,
　　　　And it is meet I presently set forth.　　　　400
DUKE I am sorry that your leisure serves you not.
　　　　Antonio, gratify this gentleman,
　　　　For in my mind you are much bound to him.
　　　　　　　　　　　　　Exit Duke and his train
BASSANIO Most worthy gentleman, I and my friend
　　　　Have by your wisdom been this day acquitted　　405
　　　　Of grievous penalties, in lieu whereof
　　　　Three thousand ducats due unto the Jew
　　　　We freely cope your courteous pains withal.
ANTONIO And stand indebted over and above
　　　　In love and service to you evermore.　　　　410

Portia refuses money, but asks insistently for Bassanio's ring: the very one she gave him as a token of her loyalty. Bassanio cannot part with it, and Portia mocks him.

1 Nerissa's smiles (in groups of three)

Unlike Bassanio and Antonio, Nerissa and the audience know Portia's true identity. Two people read aloud the whole of the opposite page; the third stops them at lines or phrases which might bring a smile to Nerissa's lips. Several of Portia's remarks have much greater significance for Nerissa than for the two men. Talk about the comic possibilities such comments give to the actors on-stage.

2 Portia's lack of mercy? (in pairs)

Portia insists on having the ring (line 428). She knows its importance and the anguish its loss will cause Bassanio. Why does she deal with her husband with the same ruthlessness as she has shown to Shylock? Talk about whether she is cruel or wise in setting this test for Bassanio. Are there other explanations for her insisting on having the ring? Jot down possible reasons, and compare them with other groups.

---

delivering saving
My ... mercenary I don't care
 about money
know recognise or have sex with (a
 pun for Nerissa's benefit?)
of force ... further I must
 persuade you more

remembrance memento
trifle trinket
proclamation public
 announcement
liberal generous
scuse excuse

PORTIA He is well paid that is well satisfied;
　　　　And I delivering you am satisfied
　　　　And therein do account myself well paid;
　　　　My mind was never yet more mercenary.
　　　　I pray you know me when we meet again.　　　　　　415
　　　　I wish you well, and so I take my leave.
BASSANIO Dear sir, of force I must attempt you further.
　　　　Take some remembrance of us as a tribute,
　　　　Not as a fee. Grant me two things, I pray you:
　　　　Not to deny me, and to pardon me.　　　　　　　420
PORTIA You press me far, and therefore I will yield.
　　　　Give me your gloves, I'll wear them for your sake;
　　　　And for your love I'll take this ring from you.
　　　　Do not draw back your hand; I'll take no more,
　　　　And you in love shall not deny me this.　　　　　425
BASSANIO This ring, good sir? Alas, it is a trifle;
　　　　I will not shame myself to give you this.
PORTIA I will have nothing else but only this;
　　　　And now methinks I have a mind to it.
BASSANIO There's more depends on this than on the value.　430
　　　　The dearest ring in Venice will I give you,
　　　　And find it out by proclamation.
　　　　Only for this I pray you pardon me.
PORTIA I see, sir, you are liberal in offers.
　　　　You taught me first to beg, and now methinks　　435
　　　　You teach me how a beggar should be answered.
BASSANIO Good sir, this ring was given me by my wife,
　　　　And when she put it on, she made me vow
　　　　That I should neither sell, nor give, nor lose it.
PORTIA That scuse serves many men to save their gifts;　440
　　　　And if your wife be not a mad woman,
　　　　And know how well I have deserved this ring,
　　　　She would not hold out enemy for ever
　　　　For giving it to me. Well, peace be with you.
　　　　　　　　　　　　　　　　Exeunt [Portia and Nerissa]

Antonio persuades Bassanio to part with the ring. Gratiano brings it to Portia. Nerissa plans to set the same test for her husband by making him give her his ring too.

1 What would you have said? (in pairs)

Antonio persuades Bassanio to reward Balthazar (Portia) by handing over his ring. Bassanio gives in without comment, but what would you have said in reply to lines 445–7?

- Talk together about whether a promise to one's partner outweighs all else.
- Write your own reply to Antonio's words – in iambic pentameter, if possible.

2 Nerissa and Shylock

Nerissa is sent to Shylock's house (lines 1 and 11) for him to sign the deed of gift, naming Lorenzo and Jessica as his heirs.

- As Nerissa, write your own account of your meeting with Shylock.
- Draw up the deed that Shylock has to sign.

3 A chance to extend the joke (in pairs)

Nerissa and Gratiano are on their way to Shylock's house. Improvise their conversation. Remember: Nerissa (in disguise) has to persuade her husband to give away his ring to someone he thinks is Balthazar's clerk . . .

Let his . . . commandement weigh what he deserves plus my love against what your wife orders
presently immediately
Fair . . . o'ertane I'm glad I've caught up with you

entreat beg
I warrant I'm sure
old (line 15) incredible
outface them be cheekier than them, stare them down
tarry wait for you

ANTONIO My lord Bassanio, let him have the ring.   445
        Let his deservings and my love withal
        Be valued 'gainst your wife's commandement.
BASSANIO Go, Gratiano, run and overtake him;
        Give him the ring, and bring him if thou canst
        Unto Antonio's house. Away, make haste.   450
                              Exit Gratiano

        Come, you and I will thither presently,
        And in the morning early will we both
        Fly toward Belmont. Come, Antonio.   *Exeunt*

ACT4   SCENE 2
Venice   A street

Enter PORTIA and NERISSA

PORTIA Enquire the Jew's house out, give him this deed,
        And let him sign it. We'll away tonight
        And be a day before our husbands home.
        This deed will be well welcome to Lorenzo.

Enter GRATIANO

GRATIANO Fair sir, you are well o'ertane.   5
        My lord Bassanio upon more advice
        Hath sent you here this ring, and doth entreat
        Your company at dinner.
PORTIA   That cannot be.
        His ring I do accept most thankfully,
        And so I pray you tell him. Furthermore,   10
        I pray you show my youth old Shylock's house.
GRATIANO That will I do.
NERISSA   [*To Portia*] Sir, I would speak with you.
        [*Aside*] I'll see if I can get my husband's ring
        Which I did make him swear to keep for ever.
PORTIA Thou mayst, I warrant. We shall have old swearing   15
        That they did give the rings away to men;
        But we'll outface them, and outswear them too.
        – Away, make haste, thou know'st where I will tarry.
NERISSA Come, good sir, will you show me to this house? [*Exeunt*]

Looking back at Act 4
Activities for groups or individuals

1 A fair trial?

- Does Shylock receive a fair trial?
- Does he get a just and/or merciful punishment?
- Which character most gains your respect in the trial scene? Why?
- Which character do you respect least?

2 Antonio's last letter

Imagine you are Antonio. It is just before the trial. Write your last letter to Bassanio, to be read after your death.

3 Who is Bellario?

Bellario writes a letter as part of Portia's plan to rescue Antonio (Scene 1 lines 150–62). What impression do you gain from his words? Does he share any of Portia's family characteristics? Write a pen portrait.

4 The knife and the scales

These props are of great significance in Scene 1. Design your ideal versions of Shylock's knife and set of scales. Try to achieve theatrical impact with your design, and ensure that both items are convincing possessions of Shylock.

5 'My deeds upon my head!'

Draw a picture to represent Shylock's fateful words (Scene 1 line 202).

6 Prejudice

Run through a list of characters who appear in Act 4. Put them in order of the degree of prejudice you think they display, then rank them in order of how much you like them. Do your two lists match?

7 'Give me some lines!'

In defeat, Shylock, normally a man of many words, says little. Dustin Hoffman, an actor who played Shylock, said, 'Half-way through the trial Portia takes over and Shakespeare doesn't give me anything to say . . . if he was still alive, I'd be saying "Give me some lines!"'

You are given the chance to write one extra speech for Shylock. At what point would you include it, and what would he say?

8 Which line?

Identify the point in the script at which you think this dramatic moment occurred. In what historical period have the director and designer set this production?

*Lorenzo and Jessica are reminded by the night of famous lovers
from classical mythology. They speak, somewhat ambiguously, of their love
for each other.*

1 'The moon shines bright' (in pairs)

- Take parts and read the opposite page aloud. Concentrate on creating a mood of romance or playfulness.
- In a second reading, add to each speech a sequence of movements or gestures which illustrate the events described by the words.
- Talk together about how a director could add to the mood of the lines by stage design and lighting and the positioning of actors on-stage.

2 'In such a night . . .' (in groups of three or four)

The moon is shining brightly. Jessica and Lorenzo recall the deeds of famous lovers on such a night.

- 'In such a night' is repeated six times. Talk together about the effects that can be achieved by such repetition.
- All the stories of the lovers mentioned have echoes of tragedy, betrayal and desertion. Talk together about why Shakespeare might have included these sombre reminders in what seems to be an idyllic setting (Belmont) with two newlyweds.
- Add another pair to Lorenzo and Jessica's list of lovers and write a few lines, describing their actions, that could be incorporated into the script (for example, Romeo and Juliet? Samson and Delilah? Antony and Cleopatra? Popeye and Olive Oyl?)
- Do some research to discover in which other plays Shakespeare wrote about Troilus, Cressida, Thisbe, Dido. Write a paragraph describing the difference in the ways in which Shakespeare treated their stories.

Troilus son of King Priam of Troy, betrayed by his lover Cressida
Thisbe frightened by a lion, she never met her lover Pyramus
Dido Queen of Carthage, deserted by Aeneas
waft beckoned to

Medea she ran away with her lover, Jason, but was deserted
Aeson Jason's father
unthrift generous
shrew small mouse-like animal, or a bad-tempered woman
outnight go on, outlast

ACT 5 SCENE I
Belmont Portia's garden

Enter LORENZO and JESSICA

LORENZO The moon shines bright. In such a night as this,
        When the sweet wind did gently kiss the trees,
        And they did make no noise, in such a night
        Troilus methinks mounted the Troyan walls
        And sighed his soul toward the Grecian tents,   5
        Where Cressid lay that night.
JESSICA   In such a night
        Did Thisbe fearfully o'ertrip the dew,
        And saw the lion's shadow ere himself,
        And ran dismayed away.
LORENZO   In such a night
        Stood Dido with a willow in her hand   10
        Upon the wild sea banks, and waft her love
        To come again to Carthage.
JESSICA   In such a night
        Medea gathered the enchanted herbs
        That did renew old Aeson.
LORENZO   In such a night
        Did Jessica steal from the wealthy Jew   15
        And with an unthrift love did run from Venice
        As far as Belmont.
JESSICA   In such a night
        Did young Lorenzo swear he loved her well,
        Stealing her soul with many vows of faith,
        And ne'er a true one.
LORENZO   In such a night   20
        Did pretty Jessica (like a little shrew)
        Slander her love, and he forgave it her.
JESSICA I would outnight you, did nobody come:
        But hark, I hear the footing of a man.

Stephano brings news of Portia's imminent return to Belmont. Lancelot informs Lorenzo that Bassanio is also on his way home. Lorenzo proposes to welcome them with music.

1 Has Portia found God? (in pairs)

Portia seems to have been very religious on her way back from Venice. She has stopped to pray at holy places and is accompanied by a holy hermit.

- Talk about possible explanations for Portia's religious behaviour after her triumph in Venice.
- Improvise a conversation between Portia and the 'holy hermit'.
- Portia is praying for a happy marriage (line 32). What do you think she would be hoping for from marriage to Bassanio? Talk about your ideas, then write a dramatic soliloquy which captures some of her hopes and dreams. You could write it in the form of a prayer.

2 Lorenzo's welcome-home party
(whole class, divided into smaller groups)

Lorenzo plans to welcome Portia home with a celebration. Remember the mood established at the opening of this scene, and the importance of Portia's return. What will the welcome be like? Talk about this, then prepare a short routine (1–2 minutes) which celebrates Portia's homecoming. You could produce a short improvised play, mime, song, music, dance or poetry, for example. Each welcoming activity can then become part of a whole-class presentation.

3 Lancelot and Lorenzo – comic confusion (in pairs)

Read lines 39–46. Here are two characters who cannot seem to find each other in the darkness! Try to memorise the lines and play the short sequence wearing blindfolds or with your eyes closed. Add a few movements and work on bringing out the humour and confusion.

Sola/Wo ha hunting cries
post messenger

expect await
signify inform people

Enter [STEPHANO,] *a messenger*

LORENZO Who comes so fast in silence of the night? 25

STEPHANO A friend.

LORENZO A friend? What friend? Your name, I pray you, friend?

STEPHANO Stephano is my name, and I bring word
 My mistress will before the break of day
 Be here at Belmont. She doth stray about 30
 By holy crosses where she kneels and prays
 For happy wedlock hours.

LORENZO   Who comes with her?

STEPHANO None but a holy hermit and her maid.
 I pray you, is my master yet returned?

LORENZO He is not, nor we have not heard from him. 35
 But go we in, I pray thee, Jessica,
 And ceremoniously let us prepare
 Some welcome for the mistress of the house.

Enter [LANCELOT,] *the Clown*

LANCELOT Sola, sola! Wo ha, ho! Sola, sola!

LORENZO Who calls? 40

LANCELOT Sola! Did you see Master Lorenzo? Master Lorenzo, sola,
 sola!

LORENZO Leave holloaing, man! Here!

LANCELOT Sola! Where, where?

LORENZO Here! 45

LANCELOT Tell him there's a post come from my master, with his horn
 full of good news: my master will be here ere morning, sweet
 soul.

LORENZO Let's in and there expect their coming.
 And yet no matter: why should we go in? 50
 My friend Stephano, signify I pray you,
 Within the house, your mistress is at hand,
 And bring your music forth into the air.

                                        [*Exit Stephano*]

Lorenzo tells Jessica of the harmony of the heavens. As the musicians play, he describes the healing powers of music.

1 Creating atmosphere (in groups of three or four)

Lorenzo's lines 54–68 describe 'the music of the spheres': the ancient belief that the moving stars made heavenly music. Explore the atmosphere his words create (for example, is it dreamlike and romantic?).

Read aloud lines 54–68, each person reading a short, meaningful unit of the script. Emphasise all the words connected with the senses. Then try other ways of reading to bring out what you feel is the mood being created here.

2 'I am never merry when I hear sweet music' (in pairs)

Jessica does not find that music cheers her, even though Lorenzo assures her of its healing powers. What causes Jessica's unresponsive mood? Talk together about what line 69 tells you of her state of mind.

3 'Music for the time doth change his nature'
(in groups of three or four)

Read Lorenzo's lines 70–88 several times. He describes the powerful effects music can have on any listener.

- Improvise a short scene to show Lorenzo's belief that music can dramatically transform frantic or brutal mood and behaviour.
- Discuss whether you agree with Lorenzo that people who cannot respond to music are villainous and untrustworthy.

4 Research the classics

Use the library to research some of Lorenzo's classical references: the music of the spheres; Diana; Ovid; Orpheus; Erebus.

Become fit
patens small plates (used at Holy Communion)
orb star
quiring singing
cherubins beautiful angels
muddy vesture of decay human body

Diana the Moon goddess
fetching mad bounds jumping
mutual stand stop all together
Orpheus a legendary Greek whose music enchanted
stockish insensitive
spoils plunder
Erebus a dark place near Hell

How sweet the moonlight sleeps upon this bank!
Here will we sit, and let the sounds of music   55
Creep in our ears; soft stillness and the night
Become the touches of sweet harmony.
Sit, Jessica. Look how the floor of heaven
Is thick inlaid with patens of bright gold.
There's not the smallest orb which thou behold'st   60
But in his motion like an angel sings,
Still choiring to the young-eyed cherubins.
Such harmony is in immortal souls,
But whilst this muddy vesture of decay
Doth grossly close it in, we cannot hear it.   65

[*Enter* STEPHANO *with musicians*]

Come, ho! and wake Diana with a hymn.
With sweetest touches pierce your mistress' ear,
And draw her home with music.
                    Music plays
JESSICA I am never merry when I hear sweet music.
LORENZO The reason is your spirits are attentive.   70
For do but note a wild and wanton herd
Or race of youthful and unhandled colts
Fetching mad bounds, bellowing and neighing loud –
Which is the hot condition of their blood –
If they but hear perchance a trumpet sound,   75
Or any air of music touch their ears,
You shall perceive them make a mutual stand,
Their savage eyes turned to a modest gaze
By the sweet power of music. Therefore the poet
Did feign that Orpheus drew trees, stones, and floods;   80
Since naught so stockish, hard, and full of rage,
But music for the time doth change his nature.
The man that hath no music in himself,
Nor is not moved with concord of sweet sounds,
Is fit for treasons, stratagems, and spoils;   85
The motions of his spirit are dull as night
And his affections dark as Erebus.
Let no such man be trusted. Mark the music.

Portia and Nerissa return, unnoticed at first, and comment on the light and the music. They discover that their husbands have not yet arrived in Belmont, and plan to keep quiet about their own absence.

1 'So shines a good deed in a naughty world'
(in groups of five or six)

Make a tableau to illustrate Portia's line 91.

2 'Nothing is good . . . without respect' (in small groups)

Talk together about whether you agree with Portia that only comparisons can reveal the true worth of anything.

3 A secret entrance (in groups of three)

Take parts and read the page opposite. Stop at the point where you think Portia and Nerissa are recognised. Work out how you would arrange the characters on-stage for this part of the scene. Remember that Lorenzo, Jessica, Stephano and the musicians are already on-stage, even though they don't speak whilst Portia and Nerissa are conversing. How, and where, do Portia and Nerissa make their entrance?

4 'Music ceases': a change of mood (in groups of five or six)

As the music stops, the whole mood of the scene changes. The characters become more businesslike. Talk together about what other theatrical devices you could use to make this transition effective and convincing on-stage.

5 What is Portia plotting?

Why is Portia so keen to ensure that no one tells Bassanio and Gratiano that their wives have been absent from Belmont? Before you read on, make some guesses about what Portia is planning. (Think about rings and disguises.)

---

naughty worthless, wicked
main of waters the ocean
respect comparison
attended in company
season appropriate time

Endymion a beautiful youth, loved
by the Moon goddess, Diana
(perhaps Portia points to Lorenzo
and Jessica, asleep)

Enter PORTIA *and* NERISSA

PORTIA That light we see is burning in my hall.
How far that little candle throws his beams!   90
So shines a good deed in a naughty world.
NERISSA When the moon shone we did not see the candle.
PORTIA So doth the greater glory dim the less:
A substitute shines brightly as a king
Until a king be by, and then his state   95
Empties itself, as doth an inland brook
Into the main of waters. Music, hark!
NERISSA It is your music, madam, of the house.
PORTIA Nothing is good, I see, without respect;
Methinks it sounds much sweeter than by day.   100
NERISSA Silence bestows that virtue on it, madam.
PORTIA The crow doth sing as sweetly as the lark
When neither is attended; and I think
The nightingale, if she should sing by day
When every goose is cackling, would be thought   105
No better a musician than the wren.
How many things by season seasoned are
To their right praise and true perfection.
Peace, ho! The moon sleeps with Endymion
And would not be awaked!
              [*Music ceases*]
LORENZO   That is the voice,   110
Or I am much deceived, of Portia!
PORTIA He knows me as the blind man knows the cuckoo
By the bad voice.
LORENZO   Dear lady, welcome home!
PORTIA We have been praying for our husbands' welfare,
Which speed we hope the better for our words.   115
Are they returned?
LORENZO   Madam, they are not yet.
But there is come a messenger before
To signify their coming.
PORTIA   Go in, Nerissa:
Give order to my servants that they take
No note at all of our being absent hence –   120
Nor you Lorenzo, Jessica nor you.

Bassanio returns with Antonio and Gratiano. Nerissa challenges Gratiano. He has given away her ring, which he swore to wear as long as he lived!

1 A change of scene? (in groups of three)

Some editors divide Act 5 into two scenes, ending Scene 1 at line 126. Talk together about why you think they choose to do this.

2 Antonio in Belmont

This is Antonio's only visit to Belmont. The traumatic experience of his trial is only recently behind him. What do you think will be in his mind as he arrives? List his thoughts. Include his reflections on the trial and his first impressions of Belmont, Portia and Nerissa.

As Antonio, write a short piece entitled 'Reflections'.

3 An argument begins (in groups of five)

There will be much embarrassment for Gratiano and Bassanio as they try to explain why they've given away their wives' rings. To enjoy the domestic quarrels, take parts as the husbands and wives and Antonio, and read quickly through to the end of the play.

4 'You do me wrong!' (in pairs)

How did the quarrel between Gratiano and his wife begin? Just how did Nerissa 'notice' that Gratiano had lost the ring? Improvise the way their conversation began and develop it as far as 'By yonder moon . . .' (line 142).

5 A puzzle

No one is quite sure what lines 127–8 mean. One suggestion is that Bassanio is complimenting Portia with the equivalent of 'You are my sunshine'. What do you think?

---

the Antipodes the other side of the world
light wanton, unfaithful
scant cut short
gelt castrated
poesy motto

cutler's poetry poor-quality verse
You should . . . respective You should have respected the circumstances under which it was given

[A tucket sounds]

LORENZO Your husband is at hand, I hear his trumpet.
　　　We are no telltales, madam; fear you not.
PORTIA This night methinks is but the daylight sick,
　　　It looks a little paler; 'tis a day　　　　　　　　125
　　　Such as the day is when the sun is hid.

Enter BASSANIO, ANTONIO, GRATIANO, *and their followers*

BASSANIO We should hold day with the Antipodes,
　　　If you would walk in absence of the sun.
PORTIA Let me give light, but let me not be light,
　　　For a light wife doth make a heavy husband,　　　130
　　　And never be Bassanio so for me –
　　　But God sort all! You are welcome home, my lord.
BASSANIO I thank you, madam. Give welcome to my friend.
　　　This is the man, this is Antonio,
　　　To whom I am so infinitely bound.　　　　　　　135
PORTIA You should in all sense be much bound to him,
　　　For as I hear he was much bound for you.
ANTONIO No more than I am well acquitted of.
PORTIA Sir, you are very welcome to our house.
　　　It must appear in other ways than words:　　　140
　　　Therefore I scant this breathing courtesy.
GRATIANO *[To Nerissa]* By yonder moon I swear you do me wrong!
　　　In faith, I gave it to the judge's clerk,
　　　Would he were gelt that had it, for my part,
　　　Since you do take it, love, so much at heart.　　　145
PORTIA A quarrel ho, already! What's the matter?
GRATIANO About a hoop of gold, a paltry ring
　　　That she did give me, whose poesy was
　　　For all the world like cutler's poetry
　　　Upon a knife: 'Love me, and leave me not.'　　　150
NERISSA What talk you of the poesy or the value?
　　　You swore to me when I did give it you.
　　　That you would wear it till your hour of death,
　　　And that it should lie with you in your grave.
　　　Though not for me, yet for your vehement oaths　　　155
　　　You should have been respective and have kept it.
　　　Gave it a judge's clerk! No, God's my judge
　　　The clerk will ne'er wear hair on's face that had it.

Gratiano insists that he gave the ring to the judge's clerk. Portia reproaches him, saying that Bassanio would never have parted with her ring. Gratiano tells Portia that's exactly what Bassanio has done.

1 Portia: a tongue-in-cheek performance
(in groups of three)

Portia and Nerissa are in a conspiracy with the audience. It's another occasion when the audience knows more than most of the other characters – in this case, Bassanio and Gratiano. Portia's lines 166–76 sound very serious to the two husbands, but are very amusing to the audience. She already has the ring in her possession, and she wants to make Bassanio squirm! Bassanio must be feeling very guilty: Gratiano is being reprimanded for the same misdeed that he has committed. His agitation comes to the surface in his aside (lines 177–8) and continues as Gratiano tells that he's given away Portia's ring.

Take parts as Portia, Bassanio and Gratiano. Read lines 161–91. As one person speaks, the other two react appropriately, especially showing the expressions that appear on the men's faces. Practise different readings and reactions. Decide which are most effective. Use pauses and timing to increase the comic impact of the sequence.

If this were a cartoon strip, what would be written in Bassanio's thought bubbles while he is listening to Gratiano giving him away to Portia?

2 Bassanio's honesty (in pairs)

When Bassanio is forced to admit that he no longer has the ring, he does so without excuses. Talk together about whether you feel that here you see a different side to his character.

---

scrubbed stunted
prating talkative

aught anything

GRATIANO He will, and if he live to be a man.

NERISSA Ay, if a woman live to be a man.   160

GRATIANO Now by this hand, I gave it to a youth,
   A kind of boy, a little scrubbèd boy
   No higher than thyself, the judge's clerk,
   A prating boy that begged it as a fee;
   I could not for my heart deny it him.   165

PORTIA You were to blame, I must be plain with you,
   To part so slightly with your wife's first gift,
   A thing stuck on with oaths upon your finger
   And so riveted with faith unto your flesh.
   I gave my love a ring, and made him swear   170
   Never to part with it, and here he stands.
   I dare be sworn for him he would not leave it
   Nor pluck it from his finger for the wealth
   That the world masters. Now in faith, Gratiano,
   You give your wife too unkind a cause of grief;   175
   And 'twere to me, I should be mad at it.

BASSANIO [Aside] Why, I were best to cut my left hand off
   And swear I lost the ring defending it.

GRATIANO My lord Bassanio gave his ring away
   Unto the judge that begged it, and indeed   180
   Deserved it too; and then the boy his clerk
   That took some pains in writing, he begged mine,
   And neither man nor master would take aught
   But the two rings.

PORTIA   What ring gave you, my lord?
   Not that, I hope, which you received of me?   185

BASSANIO If I could add a lie unto a fault,
   I would deny it; but you see my finger
   Hath not the ring upon it, it is gone.

PORTIA Even so void is your false heart of truth.
   By heaven, I will ne'er come in your bed   190
   Until I see the ring.

NERISSA   Nor I in yours
   Till I again see mine.

Portia and Bassanio spar over the missing ring. Bassanio insists that he gave it to the lawyer who saved Antonio's life. Portia declares that her revenge will be to deny this lawyer nothing.

1 A war of words (in pairs)

The first sequence of an elaborate verbal battle between Portia and Bassanio is in lines 192–208.

- Read the lines, emphasising the repetitions of 'ring'.
- Read the lines again, concentrating not on fierce argument but on skirmishing with words. Try to use 'ring' differently each time you say it. Emphasise other repetitions and echoes that are used.
- Then talk together about how your different readings yield different effects. Decide which you prefer.

2 Is Portia like Shylock?

Portia has trapped Bassanio into a bond which he has promised – but been unable – to keep. Like Shylock, she is utterly determined. Think of other similarities between Shylock and Portia. Make a list of how like and unlike Portia and Shylock are. Which do you think are more important: their similarities or their differences?

---

abate reduce
contain keep
What man . . . ceremony? No man would have taken my love-gift ring if you had really explained its significance

civil doctor lawyer
held up defended
candles stars
liberal generous

BASSANIO   Sweet Portia,
    If you did know to whom I gave the ring,
    If you did know for whom I gave the ring,
    And would conceive for what I gave the ring,   195
    And how unwillingly I left the ring,
    When naught would be accepted but the ring,
    You would abate the strength of your displeasure.
PORTIA If you had known the virtue of the ring,
    Or half her worthiness that gave the ring,   200
    Or your own honour to contain the ring,
    You would not then have parted with the ring.
    What man is there so much unreasonable,
    If you had pleased to have defended it
    With any terms of zeal, wanted the modesty   205
    To urge the thing held as a ceremony?
    Nerissa teaches me what to believe:
    I'll die for't, but some woman had the ring!
BASSANIO No by my honour, madam, by my soul
    No woman had it, but a civil doctor,   210
    Which did refuse three thousand ducats of me,
    And begged the ring, the which I did deny him,
    And suffered him to go displeased away,
    Even he that had held up the very life
    Of my dear friend. What should I say, sweet lady?   215
    I was enforced to send it after him;
    I was beset with shame and courtesy;
    My honour would not let ingratitude
    So much besmear it. Pardon me, good lady,
    For by these blessèd candles of the night,   220
    Had you been there I think you would have begged
    The ring of me to give the worthy doctor.
PORTIA Let not that doctor e'er come near my house.
    Since he hath got the jewel that I loved
    And that which you did swear to keep for me,   225
    I will become as liberal as you;
    I'll not deny him anything I have,
    No, not my body, nor my husband's bed:
    Know him I shall, I am well sure of it.

Bassanio begs forgiveness, swearing always to be faithful. Portia mocks him;
Antonio tries to help him. The rings are returned, but the teasing of
Bassanio and Gratiano continues.

1 Is Bassanio grovelling? (in pairs)

Take it in turns to read aloud Bassanio's two speeches (lines 240–3
and 246–8). The first reader makes the words as oily and wheedling
as possible. The second reader concentrates on being sincere and
penitent. Which version works best?

Argus a monster with a hundred eyes	**miscarried** been lost
be well advised take care	**advisedly** knowingly
mar . . . pen castrate him	**lay/lie** slept with
double false	**in lieu of** in return for
of credit! to believe! (Meant ironically)	**cuckolds** men with unfaithful wives
	ere before

Lie not a night from home. Watch me like Argus.   230
If you do not, if I be left alone,
Now by mine honour which is yet mine own,
I'll have that doctor for my bedfellow.

NERISSA And I his clerk; therefore be well advised
How you do leave me to mine own protection.   235

GRATIANO Well, do you so. Let not me take him then,
For if I do, I'll mar the young clerk's pen.

ANTONIO I am th'unhappy subject of these quarrels.

PORTIA Sir, grieve not you; you are welcome notwithstanding.

BASSANIO Portia, forgive me this enforcèd wrong;   240
And in the hearing of these many friends
I swear to thee, even by thine own fair eyes
Wherein I see myself –

PORTIA   Mark you but that?
In both my eyes he doubly sees himself:
In each eye one. Swear by your double self,   245
And there's an oath of credit!

BASSANIO   Nay, but hear me.
Pardon this fault, and by my soul I swear
I nevermore will break an oath with thee.

ANTONIO I once did lend my body for his wealth,
Which but for him that had your husband's ring   250
Had quite miscarried. I dare be bound again,
My soul upon the forfeit, that your lord
Will nevermore break faith advisedly.

PORTIA Then you shall be his surety. Give him this,
And bid him keep it better than the other.   255

ANTONIO Here, Lord Bassanio, swear to keep this ring.

BASSANIO By heaven, it is the same I gave the doctor!

PORTIA I had it of him; pardon me, Bassanio,
For by this ring the doctor lay with me.

NERISSA And pardon me, my gentle Gratiano,   260
For that same scrubbèd boy the doctor's clerk,
In lieu of this, last night did lie with me.

GRATIANO Why, this is like the mending of highways
In summer where the ways are fair enough!
What, are we cuckolds ere we have deserved it?   265

Portia reveals the truth about her deceptions and tells Antonio that three of his ships have been saved. Lorenzo and Jessica learn that Shylock will leave all his possessions to them.

1 All is revealed (in pairs)

One person reads Portia's lines 266–79. The other reacts as each character in turn. These unravellings (denouement, unknottings) of complex plots, when final disclosures are made, are a feature of many of Shakespeare's plays.

2 More letters!

Portia has two letters. One is from Bellario, explaining her part in the trial. The other is to Antonio (but from whom?), giving him good news about his ships. Choose one letter and write it.

3 'Strange accident' (in groups of three or four)

'You shall not know by what strange accident
I chancèd on this letter.'

Portia is very secretive about how she intercepted the letter giving good news to Antonio, and about when she got it. (If news of the argosies was received before the trial, the trial should not have happened and she made a fool of everyone.) Can you solve the mystery? Make up a short play about how the letter fell into Portia's hands.

4 Shylock's legacy

Nerissa's final words tell us that Shylock has committed himself by 'deed of gift' to leave all his wealth to Lorenzo and Jessica when he dies. Produce the actual document which Nerissa hands to Lorenzo.

---

soon quickly
road anchor in harbour
manna heavenly food

charge . . . inter'gatories be examined under oath

PORTIA Speak not so grossly; you are all amazed.
Here is a letter, read it at your leisure;
It comes from Padua, from Bellario.
There you shall find that Portia was the doctor,
Nerissa there her clerk. Lorenzo here   270
Shall witness I set forth as soon as you,
And even but now returned; I have not yet
Entered my house. Antonio, you are welcome;
And I have better news in store for you
Than you expect. Unseal this letter soon;   275
There you shall find three of your argosies
Are richly come to harbour suddenly.
You shall not know by what strange accident
I chancèd on this letter.
ANTONIO   I am dumb.
BASSANIO Were you the doctor and I knew you not?   280
GRATIANO Were you the clerk that is to make me cuckold?
NERISSA Ay, but the clerk that never means to do it,
Unless he live until he be a man.
BASSANIO Sweet doctor, you shall be my bedfellow;
When I am absent, then lie with my wife.   285
ANTONIO Sweet lady, you have given me life and living;
For here I read for certain that my ships
Are safely come to road.
PORTIA   How now, Lorenzo?
My clerk hath some good comforts too for you.
NERISSA Ay, and I'll give them him without a fee.   290
There do I give to you and Jessica
From the rich Jew, a special deed of gift
After his death of all he dies possessed of.
LORENZO Fair ladies, you drop manna in the way
Of starvèd people.
PORTIA   It is almost morning;   295
And yet I am sure you are not satisfied
Of these events at full. Let us go in,
And charge us there upon inter'gatories,
And we will answer all things faithfully.

It is almost dawn as the characters go into Portia's house. Gratiano looks forward to going to bed with Nerissa, determined never again to relinquish her ring!

1 Questions . . .

As the characters prepare to leave the stage, Portia promises to 'answer all things faithfully'. Make up a question that each character in the play wishes to ask her about what has been going on.

2 Gratiano has the last word (in pairs)

- Talk together about why Gratiano, rather than another major character, concludes the play.
- You may not agree with Shakespeare's choice of Gratiano. If you disagree, which other character would you prefer? Give your reasons.
- If you think another character should deliver the final lines, write a suitable speech to end the play in what you feel is an appropriate style.
- The final lines are in rhyming couplets. Why do you think Shakespeare uses this style to end the play?

3 Final words (in groups of three or four)

Read again what each character says in her/his final lines. Talk about whether you think the speeches reveal something important about each character.

Jessica is silent. What is she thinking?

4 Curtain! Lights fade (in groups of four to eight)

Don't forget Shylock!

One production ended with an image of Shylock at prayer after Gratiano's speech. Another had Jessica left alone and desolate on stage as all the Christians had gone off ignoring her. What final impression would you wish to create? Present a tableau of the final moment of your ideal performance.

---

inter'gatory question
sore much

GRATIANO Let it be so. The first inter'gatory   300
    That my Nerissa shall be sworn on is:
    Whether till the next night she had rather stay,
    Or go to bed now, being two hours to day.
    But were the day come, I should wish it dark,
    Till I were couching with the doctor's clerk.   305
    Well, while I live I'll fear no other thing
    So sore as keeping safe Nerissa's ring.

Exeunt

Looking back at the play

1 Morning has broken . . .

Look back through Act 5. Pick out words and phrases that show day gradually breaking. Talk together about why the Act begins in moonlight and darkness and ends with daylight.

2 Portia: a touch of cruelty? (in pairs)

Portia goes to great lengths to establish control over Bassanio.

- In prolonging the business of the rings, is she being playful or cruel?
- Look through the list of characters on page 1 and identify who else has been on the receiving end of Portia's teasing or cruelty.
- Talk together about whether or not you think there is a cruel streak in Portia's personality.

3 To cut or not to cut . . .

If you were directing the play, would you leave in Act 5 or would you cut it altogether and end the play at the close of the trial scene?

4 Happy ever after?

Act 5 focuses on three married couples:

Portia and Bassanio
Nerissa and Gratiano
Jessica and Lorenzo

Will the marriages last? What do you think?

5 Ten years on . . . some interviews

Imagine that you are a researcher for a magazine. One of your tasks is to track down and interview some of the characters from the play ten years after the point at which it ends, and to find out how their lives have changed. Choose your characters and conduct the interviews.

6 Shylock comes to Belmont

Imagine that Shylock visits Belmont. Write about what happens.

7 Portia sells the caskets

Now that Portia has no further use for the caskets, she decides to sell them! Write or design an advertisement that she could use to help her do this.

The language of love and loyalty; of hate and prejudice

The Merchant of Venice is a story of love and hate, and both emotions are expressed powerfully in the play.

- Collect examples of the play's language of love and loyalty between lovers, friends, parents and children. What similarities and differences can you detect between how these groups express their feelings?

- The play is renowned for the bitter conflict between Jew and Christian. Collect examples of how other characters speak about Shylock. Try to identify what their words of hatred have in common.

- Collect a range of quotations which show the intensity of Shylock's dislike for Antonio. What makes this particular language so powerful?

Telling the story

There are four strands to the story of *The Merchant of Venice*:

- the bond: Shylock and the pound of flesh
- the caskets: the winning of Portia
- the elopement: Jessica and Lorenzo
- the rings: a love test.

None of these strands was Shakespeare's own invention. The 'Shylock' story was probably based on 'Il Pecorone' (The Idiot), an old Italian story. The caskets appear in an old medieval tale, and the elopement and the rings were popular stories in fifteenth-century Italy. As with nearly all his plays, Shakespeare drew on existing stories, but altered them to great dramatic effect. For example, in the original bond story it is the hero's godfather who is to be punished by losing a pound of flesh. To the casket story, Shakespeare adds his touch: Portia is restricted by her dead father's will.

- Which of the four strands has the biggest share of the script?
- Which, for you, is the most important? Why?
- Re-tell the story, but leave out each of the four strands in turn. What does the play lose or gain each time?

Write your own version!

Just as every production of *The Merchant of Venice* is different, so every re-telling of the story differs, depending on the intentions of the storyteller and the particular reader's interests. How would you tell the story? Would you try to blend all the strands together, or would you highlight some aspects and play down others? Try one or more of the following:

- re-write the play as a mini-saga (exactly fifty words)
- produce a summary of the plot concise enough to fit into a programme for a school production
- devise a pictorial version of the play which captures the story in no more than six illustrations
- a television script
- a cliffhanger: a serial, in five episodes, each one ending at a moment of climax or suspense.

Shylock: villain or victim?

The age-old dilemma about Shylock is this: is he tragic or is he comic?
And, of course, he's both. He's one of the most complex human beings
Shakespeare wrote.

(Sir Peter Hall, theatre director)

He becomes that which he most abhors. He's torn to shreds
emotionally by the society around him. He becomes the very thing that's
reduced him . . . that's taken his humanity away.

(Dustin Hoffman, actor)

There has always been controversy about Shylock. To some he is a
miserly money-lender who delights in the prospect of cutting a pound
of flesh from the noble merchant who has exposed his corrupt ways.
He is a bloodthirsty fiend armed with scales and knife, who cares
more for his money than for his runaway daughter. Such a view sees
him as a comic or malign villain who gets his comeuppance in the
end.

A quite different perspective sees him as the victim of the society
around him. Here he is a godly, clean-living family man who merely
wishes to conduct his business unimpeded. He becomes a man driven
to revenge by mindless persecution and the cruel theft of his only
child. This view casts him as a naive, misguided soul who tries to get
even within the law of those who hate him, only to be cruelly tricked
and humiliated yet again.

There's no simple answer to the question 'villain or victim?', but
the fact that Shylock has fascinated audiences for 400 years is
evidence that he is one of Shakespeare's most human and believable
characters. What follows will help you to form your own view of
Shylock, although you will detect a strongly anti-racist stance in what
we, the editors of this edition, have written. No one can be neutral
about *The Merchant of Venice*.

Where are the Jews?

Two thousand years ago the Jews were known as Hebrews or
Israelites and lived in the part of the world now known as Israel. At
that time their land was occupied by the Romans, who at first allowed
them religious freedom but later tried to crush the Jewish faith and

culture. Such persecution led many Jews to seek new lives in other countries, a process known as the Diaspora (the dispersion of the Jews). Now there are Jewish communities living all over the world.

Research the rituals and customs of the Jewish faith. You could use the school or college library, or enlist the help of Jewish friends or your religious studies teacher. What you find out will help you to understand Shylock's behaviour.

Why were the Jews persecuted?

Jews in foreign lands resolutely kept up their customs and religion. They formed tight-knit communities and became known for their intelligence, hard work and business acumen. These qualities some-times led to their being mistrusted and resented. This was especially the case in Christian countries, where anti-Jewish feeling (anti-Semitism) can still be very strong. The history of the Jews is marked by terrible hardship and atrocities. You will find that most European countries have past records of crimes against the Jews.

The greatest Jewish suffering was endured during the Nazi domination of Europe before and during the Second World War (1939–45). Under the leadership of Adolf Hitler, the Nazis took control of Germany in 1932. They persuaded many Germans that the Jews were responsible for their country's problems. With widespread popular support, the Nazi government conducted a programme of persecution and extermination of Jewish men, women and children in Germany and the other European countries it occupied. Six million Jews lost their lives during this terrible time: the period of history known starkly as the Holocaust. This appalling cruelty began with the casual everyday racism which Shylock also has to endure from the Christians of Venice.

- Study the photograph opposite, taken in the city of Munich in 1933 at the start of the Nazi domination of Germany. The man wearing the placard is a Jewish lawyer, Dr Spiegel. He had asked for police protection against the Nazis. The placard reads: 'I'll never again make any complaints to the police'.

  What similarities are there between the cases of Shylock and Dr Spiegel?
- Research the history of the Jewish community in your own country, or your own town or district. Can you find evidence of prejudice against the Jews?

How Shylock is persecuted

Shylock's treatment at the hands of his fellow Venetians is typical of the intolerance suffered by Jews over the centuries. Throughout the play Shylock suffers constant verbal abuse:

evil soul	bloody creditor
villain with a smiling cheek	inhuman wretch
misbeliever	unfeeling man
goodly apple rotten at the heart	harsh Jew
cut-throat dog	damned, inexecrable dog
stranger cur	currish spirit
fiend	wolfish, bloody, starved and
devil	ravenous
faithless Jew	cruel devil
dog Jew	Beg that thou mayst have leave to
old carrion	hang thyself
impenetrable cur.	

Work in groups of four or five. One person is seated, while the others surround her, calling out insults from the list above. No one should be subjected to this for longer than thirty seconds, but everyone should have a turn in the chair. Talk about how you felt being treated in this way, then consider the effect over time of such habitual abuse on Shylock.

Shylock's trouble with the Christians dates back to well before the start of the play. He speaks of an 'ancient grudge' when he first appears, and gives a vivid account of Antonio's racist bullying.

- Read lines 98–121 of Act 1 Scene 3 and make a full list of Antonio's insults and abuses against Shylock.

Despite the enmity between Antonio and Shylock, the Christian still does business with the Jew. Antonio is fully aware of the terms of the bond which he signs in the presence of a solicitor. Shylock makes no secret of his intentions if his enemy can't pay up at the end of three months. Then the unthinkable happens: Antonio loses all his ships, and with them his wealth. He is not only bankrupt but also trapped by his bond with the Jew. Antonio entered willingly into the deal to help Bassanio, knowing full well what the consequences might be. Nevertheless, the Christians are outraged when Shylock claims what is lawfully his.

- Collect quotations which show Christian objections to Shylock's bond before Portia intervenes.

Shylock might be accused of wishing to trap Antonio, but the Christians similarly conspire against him. They invite him to dinner on the very night a gang of them help Lorenzo steal Jessica, along with a considerable portion of his wealth. Portia also carefully plans her action against Shylock. In the trial, she waits until the very moment he is going to cut Antonio's flesh to reveal the loophole she has discovered in the bond between them. Before that she repeatedly gives Shylock the chance to back down, so adding to the humiliation she clearly wishes to inflict on him in her hour of victory. When Shylock is defeated, he is shown little of the mercy which before was so earnestly recommended to him by Portia. Half his wealth is confiscated and – far worse – he must lose his faith and convert to Christianity.

- As Portia, write your own account of your involvement in the trial. Explain your plan to rescue Antonio and defeat Shylock. Why did you show him no mercy?

How Shylock responds to prejudice

Shylock's bloodthirsty campaign against Antonio is morally indefensible. He eschews the simple purity of his normal life and degrades himself in his animal-like quest to win a pound of the Christian's flesh. His behaviour is wrong . . . but it is understandable. Shylock is a foreigner in his own city. He may have lived all his life in Venice, yet he is treated as an alien. Like his fellow Jews, he tries to rise above such prejudice and seeks security and success in money-lending. He calls this 'well won thrift'; Antonio disparagingly calls it 'interest'. Antonio and the Christians won't allow themselves to lend money for profit, but to support their extravagant lifestyles they still need money loans from the Jews they persecute. Shylock has been waiting to strike back at Antonio, one of Venice's principal anti-Semites, and sees his chance when the merchant is compelled to come to him for credit.

Significantly, Shylock tries to attack his enemy within the law of Venice. He is often at pains to point out the legality of his actions and after the loss of Antonio's ships refers obsessively and repeatedly to his 'bond'. In the trial, he openly questions the validity of Venetian justice if it is not to be enforced on his behalf. He demands that his case is dealt with according to the letter of the law, and of course this is turned harshly against him when it is revealed that he himself has behaved illegally.

- Collect Shylock's references to his legal agreement with Antonio and other comments he makes about the law. Talk together about why it is so important to Shylock to be able to use the law of Venice against Antonio.

Shylock despises Antonio from the start of the play. His hatred is intensified by the loss of Jessica, perhaps the key to his emotional reactions from then on. In his clash with Salarino and Solanio just after Jessica's elopement (Act 3 Scene 1) he claims that his suffering and anger are produced by the Christians themselves. He blames his villainy on them, arguing that it is simply imitation of their own prejudice and cruelty.

- Re-read lines 42–57 of Act 3 Scene 1. How convinced are you of Shylock's justification for his actions? Think of actual examples in history or modern times which show that racism provokes similar cruelty in its victims.

Was Shakespeare anti-Semitic?

Shakespeare's characters, notably in *The Merchant of Venice*, often express racist views, but whether Shakespeare himself was a racist is open to dispute. What is clear is that he understood the suffering and the behaviour which results from racial prejudice. Shylock's key speech in Act 3 Scene 1 is a plea of supreme eloquence for our common humanity. However, Shakespeare's handling of Shylock is deeply ambiguous. Shylock is intensely and movingly human, yet at the end he receives the same treatment as a stage villain. He leaves the court in Act 4 with hardly a word, apparently completely defeated. One would have thought that Shakespeare wouldn't want us to forget about him, but he doesn't appear in Act 5 and is barely mentioned there. If Shakespeare wanted the audience to view this central character as a victim, surely he'd give him something to say or do in the final act?

- Your school or college drama group wishes to stage *The Merchant of Venice*, but is opposed by the Head or Principal, who fears that the play might offend ethnic minority groups in the school and the local community. The Head calls a meeting for those involved. Decide who would be present and improvise this difficult encounter in front of the rest of the class. Everyone, including those observing, has the right to stop the action to ask questions, to express opinions, and to ask for or offer advice.

Shylock over the years

In the early days of English theatre, Shylock was performed to match the way he is described by his Christian enemies. In the nineteenth century Edmund Kean broke away from this widely accepted view by portraying him as intelligent and vulnerable. This began a trend towards humane, sympathetic depictions of Shylock which has continued until the present day.

- Try to arrange the opposite sequence of photographs of past Shylocks in chronological order. What do these images suggest about how these different actors portrayed him?

- In your own production, how would you want Shylock to be played? As the director, write some notes for other members of the company, justifying your ideas. Include a sketch of an appropriate costume design.

Women in Venice and Belmont

Venice is a city of contrasts: love and hate, loyalty and prejudice, wealth and poverty, justice and injustice. It is a city based on trade – not just in silks and spices, but also in human cargo: the Christians own slaves. Shylock taunts the Christians with their worst nightmare: that their slaves will marry their daughters (4.1.94). It is also a multicultural society. There is a significant Jewish community as well as an African population: Lancelot has a black girlfriend. But these ethnic minorities do not have equal rights with the Christian ruling class.

Most obviously, Venice is ruled entirely by men. Women have no role at all in trade, politics or law. It seems that they cannot even own property. As soon as Portia enters Venetian society by becoming engaged to Bassanio, she gives him all her wealth as well as her own freedom:

'This house, these servants, and this same myself
Are yours, my lord's'

Patriarchy rules in Belmont as well as Venice. Portia might be head of the household at the start of the play, but her father still controls her destiny, even from the grave. Even when she escapes from her father's will, she subjects herself immediately to her husband's authority. From now on she will be known as 'Lord Bassanio's wife' rather than Portia.

- Read through the scenes in Acts 1–3 in which women appear. Make a list of all the ways in which their lives are restricted.
- Improvise a secret meeting of the Venetian Women's Liberation Front. Your task is to compile a charter listing your demands for greater freedom for women.
- Turn to the cast list on page 1. Rank each character in order of social status as perceived by the Duke; as perceived by Jessica; as perceived by yourself.
- Look quickly at the casket scenes. Does Portia know which casket contains her portrait? Do you think she tries to influence her suitors' choices? Or is she completely at the mercy of fate?

Jessica, Nerissa and Portia

The three women in the play have very different personalities. None the less, they all marry friends of Antonio at roughly the same time and are all involved in the defeat of Shylock. Study the pen portraits below. Check how far you agree with each, then write a paragraph of your own on each of the women.

Jessica

She wishes to convert to Christianity and reject her Jewish roots; ashamed of her father, Shylock; perhaps frustrated by his over-protectiveness and killjoy attitude; becomes involved in a Christian plot and schemes against her father behind his back; she steals from him (money and jewels, including a turquoise ring of great sentimental value). She and Lorenzo are named as Shylock's heirs.

Will her life with Lorenzo be happy? Will she be fully accepted by Christian men *and* women?

Nerissa

Not exactly a servant to Portia, more a lady-in-waiting or confidante; has common sense and a sense of humour; her attitude to Portia's suitors shows that she has no illusions about men; takes orders from Portia without question; agrees to marry Gratiano (a show-off and a racist bully) after some persuasion, but has known him for only a short time.

How will she cope with such a husband?

Portia

Her name has become associated with the qualities of justice and mercy, but she is hard-hearted and calculating in her public humiliation of Shylock; strong-minded, resourceful and intelligent, but still loyally abides by the rules of the marriage lottery devised by her dead father; gives herself completely to Bassanio despite his wishing to marry her to pay off his debts brought about by an extravagant lifestyle.

Will being subservient to a man like Bassanio suit Portia?

Imagine you are a journalist for a women's magazine. It is now ten years after the point at which the play ends. For a 'Where Are They Now?' feature you decide to trace and interview the three women. Write your article, giving details of how they feel about the events of a decade before, and how their lives have changed since then.

Tensions and oppositions in
The Merchant of Venice

There are many contrasts and conflicts in *The Merchant of Venice*. One way of looking at the play is to see it as a series of tense oppositions. But Shakespeare is not the kind of playwright who will *tell* you what you should conclude about each of the issues. Instead, he lays out the conflicting viewpoints and invites you to make up your own mind.

1 Comedy and tragedy

The play seems to end on a happy note, with the resolution of the test of the rings and the celebration of marriage. But there are many darker aspects which cast shadows over that bright ending: Shylock's humiliation and anguish; Antonio's continuing sadness; Jessica's isolation in Belmont; Lancelot's treatment of his blind father; the cruel baiting of Shylock at the trial.

Make two columns, headed 'comic moments' and 'unpleasant moments'. Fill the columns with incidents from the play.

Which mood seems to have precedence?

2 Love and hate

On the one hand the play is full of love and friendship: Portia and Bassanio; Gratiano and Nerissa; Jessica and Lorenzo; a closeness between Antonio and Bassanio that prompts great self-sacrifice. On the other, bitterness and hatred are evident: Gratiano's reviling of Shylock; Shylock's coldness towards his daughter and hatred of Antonio. He sees himself as a victim of prejudice and sustains himself with his own hostility.

- In Portia's only soliloquy (3.2.108–14) she talks of the surge of love she feels for Bassanio. Think carefully about the context of her speech. Write down all the key words she uses.
- Study Shylock's first soliloquy (1.3.33–44). How does it begin to identify the nature and tone of Shylock's hatred?
- Make a drawing of a pair of scales. Place 'love' words in one scale, 'hate' words in the other. What balance results?

3 Jew and Christian

- Find examples of how important Jewishness is to Shylock.
- Find examples of Christian attitudes towards Shylock.

4 Justice and mercy

One of the central themes of the play is that of justice: the right, proper and fair treatment of individuals according to their deserts.

Read Portia's speech about mercy. Then look at the trial scene (Act 4 Scene 1). Shylock receives judgement, but does he receive justice? What qualities of mercy are displayed in this scene?

5 Venice and Belmont

To Shakespeare's contemporaries, Venice was a legendary symbol. It was renowned as a city of culture and sophisticated behaviour. More importantly, it was famous as a centre for trade and profit. It was widely believed to have a legal system which protected the rights of individuals, even when they were foreigners or 'outsiders'.

Belmont does not actually exist. It is Shakespeare's own imaginative creation, based on an idea he took from his source material. Belmont is part of a different world – or is it? It seems to be a place of beauty and grace (see the opening to Act 5), but it is riddled with prejudice against foreigners.

- Choose one scene (or part of a scene) which you feel typically represents Venetian qualities and values. Do the same for Belmont. What similarities and what differences can you discover in the two settings used by Shakespeare?

6 Appearance and reality: 'All that glisters is not gold'

The Merchant of Venice shows the danger of judging by appearances. Three female characters disguise themselves as male. The gold and silver caskets are examples of how outward show can be misleading. The device of the rings signifies betrayal, besides adding to the confusion of identities. Characters mislead or deceive each other.

- Make a list of the main characters. Write alongside each the various deceptions they practise. Who tops your list for not being what they seem? Are any characters free from the charge of deception?
- Research the history of Venice. How does its reputation (art, tolerance, law, political stability) match its reality?

The language of
The Merchant of Venice

Language changes over time

Many people reading or seeing Shakespeare for the first time find his language strange and difficult, but don't be daunted. Much of Shakespeare is easily understood, and the more experience you have, the easier it becomes. The initial difficulties aren't surprising. After all, he was writing 400 years ago, and the English language has changed greatly since then.

Changes in printing

In the seventeenth century even the way of printing Shakespeare's work was different. Here's an extract from the play as it was first printed in 1600. It will not take you long to identify the speakers and from which scene it is taken.

> *Tuball.* Yes, other men haue ill lucke to , *Anthonio* as I heard in Genowa ?
> *Shy.* What, what, what, ill lucke, ill lucke. 104
> *Tuball.* Hath an Argofie caft away comming from Tripolis.
> *Shy.* I thank God, I thank God, is it true, is it true. 108
> *Tuball.* I fpoke with fome of the Saylers that efcaped the wrack.
> *Shy.* I thank thee good *Tuball*, good newes, good newes : ha ha, heere in Genowa. 112
> *Tuball.* Your daughter fpent in Genowa, as I heard, one night fourefcore ducats.
> *Shy.* Thou ftickfta dagger in me, I fhall neuer fee my gold againe. foure fcore ducats at a fitting, foure fcore ducats 116
> *Tuball.* There came diuers of *Anthonios* creditors in my company to Venice that fweare, he cannot choofe but breake. 120†
> *Shy.* I am very glad of it, ile plague him , ile torture him, *I* am glad of it.
> *Tuball.* One of them fhewed mee a ring that hee had of your daughter for a Monky. 124
> *Shy.* Out vpon her, thou tortureft mee *Tuball*, it was my Turkies, I had it of *Leah* when I was a Batcheler : I would not haue giuen it for a Wildernes of Monkies. 128

Compare the 1600 version with the way it is presented on page 79. What differences in spelling, punctuation and fonts can you find? Write down any patterns you discover in the differences.

Words drop out of use

One of the problems that students often experience with Shakespeare's language is that words change over time, and some drop out of use. You will probably have noticed already that Shakespeare uses many words which now seem unfamiliar: 'Gramercy' (God have mercy), 'doit' (penny), 'iwis' (without doubt), 'cozen' (cheat), 'cerecloth' (shroud), 'peize' (slow down), 'eche' (add to) are just a few, and the list could go on!

Find at least ten other words in the script which are no longer in use in modern Standard English. Make a list of them, with their meanings. Then try to carry on a conversation with a partner, using as many of these unfamiliar words as you can.

Words change meaning

Some words are still used regularly, but their meanings have changed. 'Naughty' is now used normally to describe the bad behaviour of a small child, but in Elizabethan times it was a much more powerful word, meaning immoral or evil. So when Portia speaks of 'these naughty times' she is being quite serious. Similarly, the word 'presently' used to mean 'at once' or 'immediately' in Shakespeare's time, rather than the current meaning: 'shortly' or 'in the near future'.

Find five other examples of word meanings that have changed over the years. You'll find the language section at the bottom of each of the left-hand pages very useful for this.

Changes in sentence structure

It's not just individual words which have changed. At times, the word order or syntax of Shakespeare seems unfamiliar to a modern audience. For example, Antonio says 'I know not why I am so sad' rather than, as we would say, 'I don't know why I am sad'.

Take Antonio's first speech in 1.1. In pairs, re-write it, line by line, in modern English. Talk together about the differences between your order of words and his.

Now take a piece of modern English (an article from a newspaper, or even your school or college brochure, and so on) and re-write it in Shakespearian syntax!

Language and social class

The language of the rich

The convention in Shakespeare's time was for playwrights to give verse to 'high-born' characters and prose to those of a lower status. Many of the Christians in the play are wealthy and educated, so they speak mainly in verse. Just as their clothes are richly elaborate (see pages 68 and 84), their language is often similarly extravagant or high-flown.

Salarino's ships would:

'Enrobe the roaring waters with my silks'

Portia wishes:

'I would be trebled twenty times myself,
A thousand times more fair, ten thousand times
More rich . . .'

The high-status characters also display their learning in their language. Their education has been in the classical literature of Greece and Rome, so they often refer to the fantastic tales of classical mythology. Bassanio describes Portia as:

'like a golden fleece
Which makes her seat of Belmont Colchos' stand,
And many Jasons come in quest of her.'

Such literary references have the effect of making their language impressively elaborate and would add extra depths of meaning, comparing the actions of the characters to the heroes of the Ancient World. The educated members of Shakespeare's audience were familiar with such stories, would easily recognise them and would appreciate the allusions. After all, they had studied them at school.

- Collect examples of the wealthy characters' ornate use of words. As well as Antonio and his friends, Portia's suitors use the style to great effect.

- Try writing in the poetic style yourself. Take an everyday event or object (morning assembly, your English teacher's car, a sports match) and transform it with your language.

The language of the poor

The poor and uneducated in the play are represented mainly by Lancelot and old Gobbo. They always speak in prose – by convention, it would be thought out of character for them to be given verse. Lancelot's language is usually comic and fast-moving. Old Gobbo refers constantly to his Christian faith – much more so than his social superiors. With these characters, Shakespeare sticks rigidly to the language rules for social class.

- Read through the Lancelot scenes and collect brief examples of his language which show his humour and vitality. Does Lancelot's prose have distinctive rhythms?

Shylock's language

As an outsider in Venice, Shylock can't be categorised with either the wealthy or the poor Christians; therefore his language is a mixture of prose and verse.

The content of Shylock's language is markedly different from that of the Christians. His business activities are much more restrained, and he rarely mixes socially outside his own ethnic group (see 1.3. 26–31). He disapproves of the Christians' prodigal, extravagant behaviour, preferring a quiet and simple life in keeping with his strict religious faith. These characteristics are reflected in his language and intensified through the misfortunes and grief that afflict him.

While the Christians refer to the lurid stories of classical mythology, Shylock speaks of the Old Testament morality tales. These frequent references to the Bible would have been familiar to many of the Elizabethan audience who, by law, had to attend church regularly. They might also have reminded them of the extreme Protestants of the time, who also used biblical quotations in their everyday speech and disapproved of such immoral pastimes as going to the theatre!

- Collect examples of Shylock's references to the Bible. Consider what effect they may have on the audience's reaction to his character.
- Shylock often mentions lowly and domestic animals such as pigs, sheep, dogs and rats. Collect examples and work out why you think he does so in each case.
- Shylock repeats key words, especially when he is angry and excited. Find several examples. Identify how they increase the dramatic effect and show something about his character.

Language and gender

The language of the characters is determined not only by their social class but also by their gender. An important question to consider is whether there is a male way of speaking which is different from the female way. Most of the men in the play are preoccupied with matters of finance and the law. The women, though conscious of the importance of wealth, are trapped into hatching love plots on the fringes of male activities. Portia has an interest in the law, but has to resort to dressing up as a man before she can act on behalf of her husband's best friend.

- Read through the entirely male Act 1 Scene 1 and collect examples of words connected with business and commerce.

- Now read through Act 1 Scene 2 to find the main topic of the women's conversation. Can you find any other important differences between the language of the two scenes? Write an essay setting out your views, with examples, on whether or not you think there is distinctive 'men's language' and 'women's language' in *The Merchant of Venice*.

- What happens when love and money meet? In Act 1 Scene 1 Bassanio tells Antonio he regards his courtship of Portia as a way of making money. Re-read Bassanio's wooing of Portia in Act 3 Scene 2 to see if his materialism (interest in money) intrudes into their conversation. Does Portia seem to be persuaded by this way of speaking?

- What happens to language when women dress as men? Portia and Nerissa talk of adopting manly behaviour (Act 3 Scene 4) to go with their disguises for the trial. Do they also speak differently when they appear as men? Find some examples from Portia's language in the trial scene, and talk together about whether you think it is men's talk.

- When Portia returns to Belmont she has shed her disguise, but has her language changed? Re-read Act 5 to see what she has retained of Doctor Balthazar's legal mannerisms.

Shakespeare's verse

We are used to drama on film, TV or stage in which the language is very like the words we speak in our everyday lives, but in the late sixteenth century, audience expectations were different. The Elizabethans loved language, especially poetry, and it was the convention for plays to be written in verse. It was expected that the characters' words would be 'poetical' and would contain imagery, rhythm and rhyme. Remember: Shakespeare was a poet who wrote plays, so he always tried to write his verse or prose in ways that would have the greatest dramatic impact. That's another reason why his language isn't like everyday speech.

Shakespeare's verse is easy to recognise from the way it is printed. Glance quickly back through the play to remind yourself of how the verse is set out differently from the prose. His verse is in iambic pentameter. Don't be put off by its name – it's quite easy to recognise, and good fun to work on. It usually has ten syllables per line, and each line has five beats or 'stresses'. This line of Portia's is marked to show the stressed (/) and unstressed (x) syllables.

    x /   x   /   x   / x   / x   /
    Behold there stand the caskets noble prince

- Read the line aloud in unison with your partner, but pronounce every syllable very clearly, almost as if each one was a separate word. As you read, beat out the five-stress rhythm (clap hands, tap the desk, etc.).
- Now turn to lines 33–7 in Act 1 Scene 3. Repeat what you have just done. Can you find the rhythm? When you have found it, try the exercise again with some verse of another character. The choice is yours!

Obviously, you would not expect actors to speak in this very stilted way on-stage. But good verse-speakers are sensitive to the rhythm of the lines, even if it's not explicitly obvious to the listener. The rhythm makes the lines easier to learn, and – far more importantly – reinforces their meaning.

Another way of finding out how iambic pentameter works is to write some yourself. Use Shylock's bitter words about Antonio again (1.3.33–7) and model your work on them.

The play in performance

The Merchant of Venice was first performed in 1596 or 1597, but very little is known about productions in Shakespeare's time. What can be guessed is that those first audiences had in their minds Christopher Marlowe's hugely successful *Jew of Malta*, in which a stereotypical villainous Jew performed all kinds of outrages. They would also probably think of Dr Lopez, the Jewish doctor who had been executed for allegedly trying to poison Queen Elizabeth.

The play was virtually neglected throughout the seventeenth century, but in 1701 George Granville re-worked the script as *The Jew of Venice*. He virtually re-wrote the play, promoted Shylock to the title role, and made him a comic figure. Many of the 'minor' characters were removed. But Shakespeare's own play returned to the stage in 1741, and for the next 150 years it became a star vehicle for leading actors playing Shylock.

Most productions in the nineteenth century truly made it Shylock's play, presenting him as a tragic figure, powerful, passionate and often tormented. Performances often cut Act 5 altogether, ending the play with Shylock's defeat. In the first half of the century the actor Edmund Kean in particular was hugely successful in the role. Later in the century, Henry Irving's production (1879) focused sympathetically on Shylock's inherent dignity and nobility, presenting him in a positive light.

In the twentieth century theatrical attempts to realise the full complexity of Shakespeare's play have been accelerated by the appalling treatment Hitler and the Nazis meted out to the Jews. Nazis even used Shakespeare as part of their propaganda. In 1943 Baldur von Schirach, the Nazi governor of Vienna, ordered the local theatre to mount a production of *The Merchant of Venice*. The actor Werner Krauf played Shylock as 'loathsome, strange and amazingly horrible, crawling across the stage'. Of course, there is no justification in Shakespeare's script for such a gross distortion. Since the Holocaust, every production has had in some way to take account of the terrible fate of the Jews under Hitler. Modern productions usually take an overtly anti-racist stance, with Shylock sometimes hardly different in appearance from his fellow citizens but still subject to being spat upon by the Christians.

Other contemporary concerns have characterised modern productions. An overtly homosexual relationship between Antonio and Bassanio has been stressed. Portia has appeared as an active agent of the Women's Liberation Movement. And Lorenzo, who has some of the most lyrical poetry in the play, has been portrayed as a dull, unromantic pedant.

Visit a production of
The Merchant of Venice

Prepare for and follow up a visit through one or more of the following:

- Everyone chooses a character (or an incident or a scene) to watch especially closely. Write down your expectations before you go. Report back to the class on how your expectations for 'your' character or scene were fulfilled or challenged.

- Compare the production with another that you have seen on film or video. How did the settings differ? Were any parts of the script omitted or re-arranged? Was there any significant difference in the ways in which the characters were presented? Which themes or issues were stressed?

- Write your own review. Record your own response to what you actually saw and heard. Be specific about different aspects of the production: casting, costumes, and the way the lines were delivered.

Most importantly – enjoy it!

Staging the play

The popular image aroused by Venice is a city of canals, gondolas, bridges and palaces, a city steeped in history and culture. Belmont conjures up visions of a great country house or estate set in expansive grounds, a sophisticated and opulent location.

It was a feature of nineteenth-century productions of *The Merchant of Venice* to use these stereotypical settings, to make the locations as realistic and authentic as possible. The twentieth century, however, has seen a wider range of interpretations. The Royal Shakespeare Company's production in 1932 evoked a 'dreamlike' or surreal atmosphere, enhanced by costumes which were a mix of different periods and styles. In contrast, Jonathan Miller's 1970 production for the National Theatre was meticulously set in the 1880s and had a distinctly Victorian atmosphere. The English Shakespeare Company's 1991 production was set in 1930s Fascist Italy, complete with concentration camp watchtowers and Jews being burned in effigy.

Below is a photograph of the set for the 1987 production by the Royal Shakespeare Company. Talk together about how you would adapt this set to represent the three locations needed for the play (Venice, Belmont and the courtroom). Remember that each scene needs to flow swiftly into the next.

If, as in some eighteenth-century productions, Act 5 were deliberately omitted, and the play ended with Shylock's exit, what would it gain and what would it lose?

Stage your own production of
The Merchant of Venice

Talk together about the period and place in which you will set your play. Clearly, any historical setting, particularly one that is post-Holocaust, will have significant resonances. Then choose one or more of the following activities.

- Design the basic set. If your production is going to be school-based, you will need to work with a particular space in mind (either indoors or outdoors). Decide where you want the audience to be seated. Consider whether you want a thrust stage or whether you want to present the play 'in the round'. Sketch your set or make a three-dimensional model of it. Work out how you will use the set to depict the three different locations: Venice, Belmont and the courtroom.

- Design the costumes. Study some of the ways Shylock has been presented (see page 173). Think about the three disguises needed. Draw contrasting pictures of Portia as herself and then as Doctor Balthazar.

- Design the props. Two important ones are the scales and the knife, used in the trial scene. What about the caskets?

- Design a sound programme to accompany any one scene.

- Design a publicity poster. Use illustrations and language that make people take notice

- Design the programme. It could include a summary of the plot, a cast list, interviews with the actors, a history of recent productions and rehearsal photographs.

- Cast the play. Suggest people at your school or college, or from the world of TV, theatre or the media.

- Choose any scene from the play and produce your version of a director's prompt book for that scene. Your prompt book should include detailed notes about the ways in which you want the actors to perform the script, notes on the setting and props, on entrances and exits – anything, in fact, that will help you to bring that scene to life!

William Shakespeare 1564–1616

1564 Born Stratford-upon-Avon, eldest son of John and Mary Shakespeare.
1582 Married to Anne Hathaway of Shottery, near Stratford.
1583 Daughter, Susanna, born.
1585 Twins, son and daughter, Hamnet and Judith, born.
1592 First mention of Shakespeare in London. Robert Greene, another playwright, described Shakespeare as 'an upstart crow beautified with our feathers . . .'. Greene seems to have been jealous of Shakespeare. He mocked Shakespeare's name, calling him 'the only Shake-scene in a country' (presumably because Shakespeare was writing successful plays).
1595 A shareholder in 'The Lord Chamberlain's Men', an acting company that became extremely popular.
1596 Son Hamnet died, aged eleven.
      Father, John, granted arms (acknowledged as a gentleman).
1597 Bought New Place, the grandest house in Stratford.
1598 Acted in Ben Jonson's *Every Man in His Humour*.
1599 Globe Theatre opens on Bankside. Performances in the open air.
1601 Father, John, dies.
1603 James I granted Shakespeare's company a royal patent: 'The Lord Chamberlain's Men' became 'The King's Men' and played about twelve performances each year at court.
1607 Daughter, Susanna, marries Dr John Hall.
1608 Mother, Mary, dies.
1609 'The King's Men' begin performing indoors at Blackfriars Theatre.
1610 Probably returned from London to live in Stratford.
1616 Daughter, Judith, marries Thomas Quiney.
      Died. Buried in Holy Trinity Church, Stratford-upon-Avon.

The plays and poems
(no one knows exactly when he wrote each play)

1589–1595 *The Two Gentlemen of Verona, The Taming of the Shrew, First, Second and Third Parts of King Henry VI, Titus Andronicus, King Richard III, The Comedy of Errors, Love's Labour's Lost, A Midsummer Night's Dream, Romeo and Juliet, King Richard II* (and the long poems *Venus and Adonis* and *The Rape of Lucrece*).

1596–1599 *King John, The Merchant of Venice, First and Second Parts of King Henry IV, The Merry Wives of Windsor, Much Ado About Nothing, King Henry V, Julius Caesar* (and probably the *Sonnets*).

1600–1605 *As You Like It, Hamlet, Twelfth Night, Troilus and Cressida, Measure for Measure, Othello, All's Well That Ends Well, Timon of Athens, King Lear.*

1606–1611 *Macbeth, Antony and Cleopatra, Pericles, Coriolanus, The Winter's Tale, Cymbeline, The Tempest.*

1613 *King Henry VIII, The Two Noble Kinsmen* (both probably with John Fletcher).

1623 Shakespeare's plays published as a collection (now called the First Folio).